Mom Christmas

A Book of Days

Bertha Catherine Madott

A Book of Days

Reflections Inspired by the Liturgical Year

NOVALIS

Cover design and layout: Gilles Lépine
Artwork: Nina Price

Business office: Novalis, P.O. Box 990, Outremont, Quebec H2V 4S7
Printed in Canada

Canadian Cataloguing in Publication Data

Madott, Bertha Catherine, 1948-

A book of days: reflections inspired by the liturgical year

ISBN 2-89088-551-8

1. Church year meditations. 2. Catholic Church—Liturgy—Meditations. I. Title

BX2182.2.M33 1992 242'.3 C92-090256-1

In memory of my father,
Henry Joseph Madott.
He shared his faith
with his family.

Contents

Illustrations

Preface

To write about the many wonderful days in the liturgical year, or about some of the important saints who have been honoured for generations, is impossible without occasionally using words and expressions that are not part of everyday language. While working on this little book, I discovered that even faithful and devout churchgoers are not always familiar with the technical terms that scholars and theologians may take for granted. For this reason, there are a few short and, I hope, interesting footnotes to explain some of these unusual words, ideas and images. Furthermore, the history of language is fascinating in itself, and I have tried to show how some of these perhaps strange-sounding words originally came to be. The notes also include short descriptions or explanations of customs and traditions that may be unfamiliar.

Bertha Catherine Madott
Toronto, 1992

First Sunday of Advent

First Sunday of the Liturgical Year

The Church has had a hard time making up its collective mind about the season of Advent. Should this be a time of penance and austerity to purify us before the celebrations of Christmas? In ages past, this was the approach in many Northern countries. Sometime before December 25, the devout would begin observing days of fast and abstinence, along with lengthy sessions of prayer, in preparation for the great feast.

On the other hand, should the time of Advent be a season of joy and festivity, in anticipation of the celebration at Christmas? The ancient Church in Rome seemed to favour this view and, for hundreds of years, the liturgy emphasized the happiness we experience in the days leading up to the Christ Child's birthday. Sometime in the twelfth century, the two traditions were combined, and we now have a month-long season without one definite, clear-cut, easily grasped theme.

In the secular world, there has been a most definite and pronounced commitment to the joyful side of Advent as school pageants, gift giving, holiday trips and treats of all kind predominate. A few cynical souls might claim that last-minute shopping in crowded stores is just a modern version of penance, but these voices are usually drowned out by the din of merrymakers (probably coming home from the annual office party).

How can we make sense of all this? Of course, the very meaning of "advent," with its heightened expectation of someone "coming," gives us a few clues. The most obvious aspect can be found in the event we are planning to celebrate at Christmastime itself: the birth of the babe in the manger at Bethlehem. In the weeks before Christmas, we also find ourselves thinking about the more personal form in which Jesus, as our Redeemer, acts in the lives of each one of us in the here and now. And finally, there is the long-awaited "second coming" of Christ, a heavenly king already on the way to take final possession of his kingdom.

The scripture readings over the four Sundays of Advent emphasize these three vigils. There are passages from Old Testament prophets pointing to the coming of the long-promised redeemer from the house of David. Other New Testament lessons sum up in a nutshell the challenge facing all Christians every day: the command to love one another. And there are the references, in apocalyptic terms, to the fulfilment of all things when the Son of Man comes again in glory.

No doubt there are many other helpful readings, liturgical observances and private prayers to complement these three great themes of anticipation, past, present and future.* Why then is Advent such a troublesome time of year for so many of us? The problem is certainly not the lack of material suitable to the season, but rather the overabundance of distractions associated in the modern mind with the "keeping of Christmas." Nor is it really the materialism of contemporary celebrations that is so out of touch with the Spirit of Advent, though God knows there is enough wretched excess around. Rather, the problem we face today is the frenzied compulsion to embrace so many frantic activities – the all-consuming entertainments, the never-ending preparations – all originally a source of such pleasure and satisfaction, and now turned into an exhausting obligation.

In our haste to enrich every moment of our lives, we may find that we do not have even one jot of energy left over with which to reflect on the significance of the event we are all so eagerly anticipating. Oh to be able to savour the peace of Christ for which we are preparing with such grim determination!

---

* The Advent wreath contains four candles. On the first Sunday of Advent, one of these is lit; on the second, two, and so on. An Advent calendar has 25 little pictures hidden behind tiny doors. Starting on December 1, those young at heart take great pleasure in opening one door every day, until on Christmas day they come to the picture of the Nativity. Some churches and schools put up a Nativity Tree early in December and decorate it day by day throughout the month, one ornament at a time. The best known Advent hymns are "O Come, Divine Messiah" and "O Come, O Come, Emmanuel." Concertgoers will also find many performances of Handel's oratorio, "Messiah," during this season.

The Immaculate Conception

December 8

Unlike feasts honouring "real life" events such as the Annunciation or the Visitation, this special day involves us in the commemoration of an idea. The doctrine of the Immaculate Conception, solemnly defined by Pope Pius IX in 1854 after many centuries of discussion, makes a statement about Mary's everlasting grace-filled condition, her freedom from "original sin" right from the moment of her conception, her special place as the most blessed member of humanity as redeemed by her son.*

Our understanding of Mary and her role in our salvation did not develop overnight. The New Testament authors were scarcely aware of the explosion of interest that would soon surround the mother of the Saviour, culminating in the shrines, devotions and feasts that have spread throughout the world. Furthermore, at different times, certain aspects of Mary's life have received more attention than others. The "spotless virgin untouched by sin" is a very different image than the "warm, tender and nurturing mother."

---

* The Immaculate Conception is often confused with the virgin birth. Today's feast commemorates the doctrine of Mary's lifelong freedom from sin, right from the moment of her conception. The "virgin birth" refers to the belief that Jesus, although truly a human being, was conceived without the agency of a human father. His mother gave birth to him after a normal confinement, but St. Joseph is considered his earthly father only.

When looking at Mary's exalted position in past ages, it is very easy to understand the criticism levelled at this "cult" by Protestant reformers and liberal Catholic thinkers alike, for the enormous shadow cast by Mary over all aspects of salvation tended to block out everything else, including her Son. Somehow or other, we began to imagine Christ as a virtually implacable Ruler bent on judgment and justice, and only through the mercy and intercession of his mother could we poor sinners expect to receive any hope of salvation. "Everything through Mary" became the rallying call of the devout.

The pendulum has swung the other way now, and Mary's role is sometimes minimized; popular devotion has faded in many places; "Our Lady" has moved away from the centre stage of religious attention, as she herself would have wanted it. Nevertheless, in focussing exclusively on Christ, we risk forgetting Mary, both as a symbol and as a unique human being.

The traditions of the faithful virgin, the loving mother and the ever-blessed lady, are all well-known representations from popular piety of the past. Less well understood but equally valuable is the idea of Mary as a symbol of the Church itself. If she has been singled out for special attention through her grace-filled state, so has the Church, the gathering of God's chosen people. If she has responded in faith to God's call, so has the Church, the living witness to God's presence on earth. If she has been the recipient of God's love in a special way, so has the Church, the bride waiting for her wedding feast to begin.

The "Church," as we have lately come to understand, is vastly greater than the sum of its parts. It is not just a collection of the higher clergy living in some palace in Vatican City. *We* are the Church and, however weak, misguided or unfaithful we may be as individuals, together we form a body joined to Christ, working with him and redeemed through him. And we now recognize that devotion to Mary no longer needs to be a substitute for understanding. Instead, with the sacraments, the sacred scriptures and the traditions of our faith, this devotion can be another link in the strong, pliable chain which joins us all to one another, stretching backwards and forwards in time and space for as far as we can see.

Third Sunday of Advent

December is the perfect month for enjoying the many fanciful Christmas stories that are so well suited to the short sharp days and early evenings that draw us closer to the light and warmth of our homes as the cold weather sets in. The season of the winter solstice,* the time surrounding the "day of the longest night," has long been associated with myth, legend and ritual, perhaps less so now that we can banish the darkness and gloom at the flick of a light switch, but lingering on in many of the tales that we return to year after year in our delight.

The true "winter's tale," like the nativity story itself, combines folk elements, a healthy dose of the supernatural and a heartfelt universal message, the whole cheerfully wrapped up in one optimistic, inspiring package. Drawing on these traditions, sacred and secular, are a host of Christmastime stories, including that perennial favourite by Charles Dickens, *A Christmas Carol.* Whether we read it aloud to little ones as a bedtime treat, or enjoy one of Hollywood's many screen adaptations, or perhaps best of all, indulge our grown-up selves in front of the fireplace, glass of eggnog in hand, many of us find that we never tire

---

* The winter solstice, the day in the year with the longest night, occurs around December 21. After this, the length of daylight begins to increase, slowly at first, then more dramatically towards summer. The equivalent day in summer is June 21, when the night is shortest.

of that cast of highly memorable Londoners. Scrooge's pathetic childhood memories, the Cratchits' meagre but delicious dinner, the Fezziwigs' wonderful party – these splendid Victorian set pieces never stale.

Many of us wait all year for the chance to surround ourselves with all these images of holiday plenty and celebration, but even if our tastes don't run to Dickens, there are many similar sources of Yuletide sentiment beguiling us at every corner. O. Henry's story, "The Gift of the Magi"; "The Nutcracker" ballet; Bing Crosby singing "White Christmas" – these and a galaxy of other works, whether popular, old-fashioned, silly or inspiring, all set forth a message of peace and goodwill, combined with sheer childlike pleasure, in this the season of our saviour's birth.

One hates to whisper even the softest discordant note in a setting thus bedecked with holly, mistletoe and good cheer. For once in our long year of struggle and labour, have we not earned the right to be children again, for a little while at least, with a child's spontaneous excitement and unchallenged expectations? And a child's blessed freedom from responsibility?

Perhaps we should ask Dickens, that master story teller, to answer these distasteful questions for us, and let him recall the darker shadows that we seek to avoid, shadows he himself set forth alongside his rich tableaux of innocent holiday pleasures. It is the vision presented to a shivering Scrooge by the ghost of Christmas present, the two ragged children, ugly in their fear and distress, silent witnesses at every Christmas fairy tale ever told: the twin scourges of Ignorance and Want.

We can be like the unfortunate Jacob Marley and refuse the many opportunities to share in the sufferings and concerns of the multitudes on our every side. And however ill the world fares from this lack of generosity, we will suffer even more as our spirit shrinks within us. Or we can look ignorance and want squarely in the face and do the little we can, each in our own way, starting perhaps with this very Christmas season.

And as Tiny Tim said, "God bless us every one!"*

* The Third Sunday of Advent is also characterized by the lighting of the rose-coloured candle in our Advent wreaths. The three violet ones use the traditional colour of penance. In contrast, the rose symbolizes rejoicing. The previous name for this Sunday was *Gaudete*, meaning "rejoice."

Christmas Eve

December 24

It gets dark early on December 24. By six o'clock there are few cars left on the road; storekeepers and pedestrians alike breathe a sigh of relief that the holiday shopping season is over for another year. The red and green lights decorating the buildings on our downtown streets burn brightly but there are few people around to see them. It is time for us to return to our homes, and whatever is done or undone – whether the gifts are under the tree or still being wrapped; the cookies baked or merely imagined – our preparations are now officially finished. There is very little else we can do to increase our own or anyone else's enjoyment of the season, and it is time for the celebrations to begin.

Perhaps we plan to set out a special Christmas Eve dinner lovingly recreated from Old World recipes and traditions;* perhaps we need to get the youngsters ready for midnight mass with the grown-ups this year; perhaps we want to spend some time just watching the lights twinkling on our own lavishly decorated tree. However and

* Cultures around the world mark Christmas Eve in many ways. Italian tables are always set with elaborate fish dinners on this night; the menu could include several kinds of salt cod, pasta served with anchovies or clams, and other regional seafood specialties. The Polish *vigilia*, also a meatless meal, might feature beet broth, mushroom dumplings and other hearty dishes. Closer to home, French Canadians enjoy the *tourtière*, a savoury pork pie, as part of a dinner traditionally eaten after midnight mass.

whatever we have decided to do on this blessed eve, the child within us feels the excitement all around, for Christmas is finally here!

Maybe we also have our share of regrets about good intentions gone astray this holiday season. Perhaps we ate too many Christmas treats, had too much to drink at the office party, spent too much on gifts. Perhaps we devoted little or no time to our own needs for peace and quiet, and instead distracted ourselves with a constant stream of extravagance and foolish nonsense. We may even have used the season as an excuse for our own miserable and surly behaviour when we were overwhelmed by the pressure to be perfect – the perfect host, the perfect lover, the perfect parent. How eternally frustrating it is being this limited, fragile creature tied to the earth yet hearing those choirs of heavenly voices!

But it is Christmas Eve after all, the best night of the year, the one night when we yearn to wrap ourselves up in the glow created by the good tidings, beautiful decorations and delicious treats that do seem to require so much organization every December. Yet if our Christmas cards went out late again this year, the Christ Child doesn't mind; he will be there whether we took the time to invite him or not. Maybe we forgot to buy a present for our least favourite aunt; something will turn up and meanwhile the Infant Jesus has brought us all some wonderful gifts to unwrap, including peace, love and forgiveness. Even if we spent the last four weeks saying "bah, humbug," lamenting the crass commercialism of our society and generally acting like a grouch, the babe in the manger doesn't care.

We have him with us anyway, even if we didn't put up a crib, a tree, or a stocking on the mantlepiece.

He has brought us a message, and whether we listen to it eagerly in a house decked to the rafters with cedar boughs and velvet ribbons, or whether we hear it grudgingly in a room that bad temper neglected to decorate, we can return to it each and every day of the year. Like the world's greatest Christmas present, something we always wanted and could never imagine receiving except in our wildest, most indulgent dreams, this message is always waiting for us. The messiah has finally come, and not just to save us *from* our sins, our greed and our pride, all the failings that we recognize in ourselves and those around us. He has come to save us *for* a life of eternal joy, a life that we will one day in the fullness of time understand and appreciate with every last drop of love and energy that we can muster. This Christmas Eve is really but a taste of the wonderful day to come when we will join that heavenly host and sing out with a new voice, "Glory to God in the Highest." And in the meantime, may there be peace to all people of good will here on earth.*

---

* Christmas is a "holy day of obligation," a day of great splendour and importance in the liturgical year. We are encouraged to regard this day as we would any Sunday by attending mass and devoting some of our energy to the rest and relaxation appropriate to its celebration. The other "holy day of obligation" in Canada is January 1, the Solemnity of Mary. The list of days varies from country to country.

St. Stephen the First Martyr

December 26

The apostles' mission to the world began almost immediately after Jesus Christ departed this earth. Inspired by the Good News, their preaching quickly bore fruit in the form of many new converts. In fact, it soon became impossible for the Twelve to minister adequately to all these believers, and thus they decided to choose, as their assistants, seven disciples noted for their learning and holiness. The scriptures describe for us the way in which the apostles conferred their authority on these seven new helpers through prayer and "the laying on of hands," actions used in ordination ceremonies ever since.

These seven became what we now call the first deacons, a title derived from a Greek word meaning "servant." Stephen, "a man full of faith and the Holy Spirit," was the first of these new ministers, and the picture painted of him in the Acts of the Apostles is that of a learned preacher who engaged the Jewish priests and scholars in provocative debate at the Temple. So challenging, even threatening, were his words that he was eventually dragged out of the city and stoned to death, thereby earning distinction as the first Christian martyr.

We are so familiar with stories of the early martyrs – Christians being fed to lions in the Colosseum and other tales – that we often forget the real meaning of the word.

"Martyr" in Greek originally signified a "witness," and those who die for their beliefs can surely be said to have acted as witnesses for that faith. Usually, however, our emphasis settles not on their faith but on the pious traditions of fortitude that have surrounded these heroic events.

And while we're busy checking up on the real meanings of old words, let's not forget that the official "martyrology" contains not just those whose faith was tested unto death but other saints as well. It seems that the "witness" aspect of a person's life is the deciding factor after all, more important than what we call "martyrdom."

And "saint" – we use this word today to refer to those people, usually long gone, whose lives have been examined in minute detail as part of a very careful and thorough canonization process. For the early Church, however, the "saints" included those alive and well and living nearby in the first congregations and communities dotting the Mediterranean. Paul's letters to his friends in Corinth are addressed to those "called to be saints together." And lest we think that the early Christians were more saintly than subsequent generations, we should remember that these letters are full of corrections and reproaches for those saints who were drifting away from the one true Word.

And so back to our friend Stephen.[*] Our appreciation of the life of a saint involves us in many interesting and inspiring perspectives, rather like a stroll through a green and sunny garden with detours along the way to admire the flowers, the trees and the birds. Sometimes we stop to hear a message spoken with uncommon eloquence; sometimes we are moved by good deeds, a noble life, the acts of heroism. And like the well-planned garden, there is something simple yet satisfying in our understanding of those who went before us. We have been joined together – twentieth-century observer to early Christian martyr – in a unity which we have come to call "the communion of Saints," made possible by the life of Christ, the same life which Stephen preached and witnessed.

---

[*] One of our best-loved Christmas carols, "Good King Wenceslaus," makes reference to this day, as Wenceslaus, a tenth-century Bohemian nobleman, is seen going out "on the feast of Stephen."

The Holy Innocents

December 28

This may be the only bleak day in the Christmas season. Right in the midst of our celebrations of good will, we are told a story of the massacre of children as ordered by King Herod in his fear about a new little king born somewhere in his domain. Warned of the impending disaster in a dream, St. Joseph leads his little family off to Egypt to await better days; those left behind are not as fortunate.

Mediaeval illustrations of this event were distressingly realistic – poor babies wrenched away from their horrified mothers; brutal Roman soldiers and their bloody swords and spears. Likewise Herod was always treated as one of the world's all-time great villains. A recent production of a fifteenth-century miracle play about the Christmas story emphasized this inhumanity by hiding Herod's face under a mask, half gold and half silver, turning him into a bloated, ranting sun, terrifying, remote and unreal.

This is certainly one way to look at the senseless wholesale slaughter of innocents,* whether they are babies in Galilee 2000 years ago; peasants in the Ukraine in Stalinist purges; Jews and other undesirables in the gas

---

* We are also reminded of the actions of Pharaoh in Egypt, who in his fear over the growing foreign presence in his land, orders all the Hebrew boy children to be drowned. Moses is saved from this fate by Pharaoh's daughter who finds him hidden in a water-proof cradle in the bulrushes. See Exodus 1.

chambers. "The people who were responsible must be monsters," we say; "they are not like us in any way."

Therefore, on this day which commemorates one such inhuman event, let us remember the everyday reality and say a prayer: for the children living in refugee camps the world over; the kids who are sexually assaulted in their own homes by their own relatives; the babies born with AIDS, drug addictions or syphilis; the ones who starve to death, crushed by greed and imperialism of every stripe; the millions of victims of abuse from drunken or unhinged parents; the legion who are merely neglected and left to wither like plants that are never watered; the handicapped who are not trained because the programs cost too much money; the girls who are maltreated because they turned out to be the wrong sex; the boys who are taught to use guns before they learn to read; all these holy innocents whose lives are brutalized by ordinary folks in ordinary towns and cities, while other ordinary people – not villains or inhuman monsters – somehow acquiesce in their sad fates through collective indifference, laziness and ignorance. May they all rest in peace.

The Holy Family

December 30*

There used to be a Christmas card available in museum book stores which featured a reproduction from a beautiful illuminated manuscript. In one corner, surrounded by exquisite Gothic lettering, was a miniature painting of the Holy Family: St. Joseph working with his carpenter's tools, Mary spinning thread, and Baby Jesus amusing himself in a tiny fifteenth-century playpen, a very down-to-earth trio, not at all marked by the otherworldly piety of so many other representations of them.

Other well-known illustrations of the Virgin and Child have often included an infant John the Baptist in the composition, a graphic reminder that the extended Holy Family included cousins. And the famous Leonardo Da Vinci cartoon** in the National Gallery of London shows Mary and her son practically sitting on St. Anne's lap, artistic testimony to the fact that this baby could sometimes count on the attention of grandparents.

There has been much recent emphasis on the humanity of Jesus and his natural bond to us in our adult weaknesses, temptations and longings. Long before he ever met

---

* This feast is celebrated on the Sunday in the Octave (the eight days) of Christmas. If there is no Sunday, it is observed on December 30.

** A "cartoon" is a full-sized preliminary study for a painting, fresco or other serious work of art. From the nineteenth century on, this word was also used to describe a humorous or satirical drawing.

up with the devil in the desert, however, Jesus proclaimed his link to all men, women and children by arriving on earth, not just in poverty and obscurity, but as part of a real live family, with honest-to-goodness relatives. If there is one aspect of his life that should bring us comfort and joy it is that one.

Sometimes our families shower us with support, encouragement and respect. Sometimes they are never-ending sources of frustration, guilt and repression. Some of us are blessed with a large caring network of relations; some of us are alone, orphaned, estranged, abandoned. But no matter what our circumstances, all of us had parents and grandparents, however loving or neglectful, and coming to terms with the good and bad in our upbringing is part of everyone's growing up process.

We bring our ideals about the family into a host of other relationships as well, especially towards those friends we have made throughout our lives, those whom we choose to love with all the tenderness, passion and fidelity we can muster. "She was like a sister to me," we may say. Even the wide world around us is influenced by our fundamental need for a family. Listen to our language about these virtual strangers and impersonal nation states. We talk about brothers-in-arms, our mother tongue, the fatherland.

It seems we cannot escape the importance of this most fundamental bond, either in our homes or in our public places. And as the calendar year draws to a close, instead of the desperate empty glamour of New Year's Eve, we are presented with the picture of the Holy Family, complete with relatives. If nothing else, each of us who believes can take comfort in their message of a welcome that never fails and a love that never dies.

Solemnity of Mary

January 1

If you wanted to choose just one picture to illustrate the meaning of the word "mother," what would it be? For some people, there would have to be freshly baked bread, gingham aprons and frilly curtains somewhere in the background, regardless of the features of the lady up front. Others might prefer an equally idealized version based on one of the great Renaissance madonnas, embodying perfect grace and beauty but little flesh and blood. Those whose experiences lead them into the mean streets of our cities might want to take a snapshot of a young girl, hardly much older than the bouncing youngster she's pushing along in a shabby stroller. Equally true to life would be a newsclip showing a knot of grieving women protesting the disappearance of their grown-up children under some oppressive state regime.

"Mother" certainly takes in all of these images and more – women at work in every profession from lawyer to seamstress; the whole political spectrum from right-wing world leader to militant peasant activist; those who are geniuses in the kitchen and those who are domestic catastrophes; some whom we judge to be successful, nurturing parents and a few who see themselves as inadequate failures.

On January 1, the first day of our calendar year,* we honour in a special way the Mother of God. There are many days in the year devoted to Mary and her various titles, from Sorrowful Virgin to Lady of the Rosary. Likewise some days honour special events in her life, such as the Annunciation and the Visitation. Every one of her feasts, however, and every virtue that can be attributed to her, is secondary to her role as mother of Jesus.

By "solemnity" we imply a day that is especially important in the ongoing liturgical year, one set apart in a special way to mark an event or honour a person fundamental to our history as a community of believers. And in the Solemnity of Mary, we reach beyond all the traditions that have grown up over hundreds of years – the devotions, statues, places of pilgrimage, the medals and the miracles, even the superstitions – to that which is most essential in Mary, her participation in our redemption as the mother of our saviour.

The honour accorded to her, in tribute to her role as mother, should help us in turn to value the position of mothers in each and every society, past, present and for as long as human beings will continue to be born. We all have had a fundamental need for maternal attention, yet sometimes we are tempted to take mothers in general (even our own in particular) for granted. We expect them to be there waiting to soothe us when we've been hurt,

---

* Before the Church calendar was reformed in 1970, we used to celebrate the ancient feast of the Circumcision of the infant Jesus on this day. The Eastern churches have always focused on Mary on this Octave day of Christmas, the "eighth" day after the great feast.

comfort us when we are downhearted, rejoice with us when we are glad. How often do we spend some time in appreciation of all we have received, thanks to a mother: our life, our hopes, our future?

Motherhood today comes in many styles – wearing overalls, housedresses and business suits. If we are able to have some understanding of and reverence for Mary, we will learn something not just about Jesus and his humanity but also about ourselves and the universal human condition.

The Epiphany

January 6

Long ago, when the world still had time for such things, Christmas celebrations lasted for nearly two weeks, each succeeding day marked by the giving of gifts, a tradition we commemorate in the "Twelve Days of Christmas" carol.* Those lucky enough to be expected to exchange presents with the Sovereign had a hard task ahead of them, as not one but twelve suitable extravagances had to be found. Shakespeare's delicious comedy, *Twelfth Night,* first performed for Queen Elizabeth I around 1600, conjures up the slightly exotic celebrations of the Renaissance. Those were the good old days, when honest folks sang the Boar's Head Carol; celebrated with the Wassail Bowl; set their tables with highly spiced foods and heavy wines; and decked their halls with holly, ivy and mistletoe! Gold, frankincense and myrrh were probably more common in Elizabethan England than in downtown Toronto today.

Some Europeans still enjoy the tradition of gifts on January 6. Italian children wait for the arrival of *La Befana,* the good-natured witch whose name is obviously

* The twelve days fall between Christmas and the Epiphany. Some people are confused by this carol and think of the twelve days as a countdown to December 25.

derived from "epiphany."* Like her colleague, Santa Claus, she comes with treats for good children; naughty ones might end up with a lump of coal instead. In Canada, however, there is an unseemly haste in some families to clean up the mess of Christmas as quickly as possible, throwing out the tree on Boxing Day, and tidying away all the chaos, however well-inspired, that takes over our households in December. People start preparing for Christmas weeks, even months in advance, and in one short day, the party is over. How sad!

And how foolish. Because for the gentiles (that is, those outside of Judaism), the Epiphany should really be special, the day that commemorates the announcement of the Good News to the wise men from the East, the symbolic representatives of the whole wide world. And the wise men's story has special poignancy today. Whether magicians, kings or scientists, the three travellers came from afar, bearing exotic gifts and searching for a king. They found him in a most unlikely place.

Lots of us are still looking for an answer too, and are not expecting to find one in a humble stable, surrounded by simple people and lowly animals. We enjoy the stories of the romantic quest, the exotic names and the presents fit for royalty. God grant that we, too, may accept the long, hard journey, the perseverance and patience, and the simple faith in the babe in the manger.

---

* "Epiphany" comes from a Greek word meaning "showing," drawing on the tradition of the Christ Child who was shown forth to the wise men on this day. Twelfth Night is the eve of this feast.

St. Thomas Aquinas

1225-1274

January 28

Time, in its relentless passage, inevitably softens the sharp edge of controversy. The scandalously innovative eventually becomes old hat, rebels join the establishment, and we have to wait for a new generation of fearless reformers to shake us from our lethargic complacency.

Today, after the centuries of reverence, some of it slavish, paid to the works of Thomas Aquinas, it takes a real act of imagination to see him once again as a rebellious youngster,* a trailblazing scholar, and a true innovator. It is equally difficult to imagine the uproar that developed when the young Thomas arrived home in the habit of a Dominican. Today, we are perfectly familiar with these mendicant friars, once so startlingly original, for the Franciscans and the Dominicans are now two of our largest religious orders.** Thomas' family was prepared for him to enter the religious life and, in view of

* His teacher, the illustrious St. Albert the Great, once defended his soon-to-be-famous pupil from the teasing of his fellow students in this way: "You call him a dumb ox; I tell you that the Dumb Ox will bellow so loud that his bellowing will fill the world."

** The "mendicant" friars are those without property rights. The term derives from the Latin "to beg" and formerly these friars would beg – literally – for their food and lodgings. At the time of their first appearance, the mendicants were considered a threat by some of the wealthy and powerful monasteries and the institutional Church.

their exalted position in society, it was expected that he might even be made an abbot of the Benedictine house at Monte Cassino. But to embrace the poverty of the *Domini canes*, the "dogs of God," to live virtually like a beggar, to tramp the roads from Naples to Paris in the company of other disreputable vagabonds – this was too much for the Aquino clan, and forceful measures were taken to dampen the young man's enthusiasm, including kidnapping and imprisonment.

To tempt the young man's unacceptable vocation, an attractive lady of easy virtue was introduced into his room, but when she was driven away with a blazing torch and even more fiery words, the Aquino family started to take Thomas a little more seriously. Eventually he succeeded in reconciling his family to his choice (it is said that his sisters helped him escape from captivity by means of a large basket and some rope) and so began the career of the man we now call the "Angelic Doctor."

Just as we have no problem today understanding the numbers of women and men who have been followers of Dominic and Francis, we have also become almost contemptuously familiar with the works of dear old Aristotle, as legions of first-year university students are annually exposed to small but indigestible chunks of his writing in introductory philosophy courses. No one considers this revolutionary any more; instead, these ancient writings are merely tolerated so that everyone can eventually get on to the really exciting stuff, found in the works of the more "modern" philosophers.

We have forgotten that, until the twelfth century, the writings of Aristotle were virtually unknown in the West, and Greek philosophy was represented almost exclusively by Plato. Thomas Aquinas, blessed with a broad education, an enquiring open mind and a capacity for clear systematic discourse, arrived on the scene in Paris at just the right moment, when enough of the new learning was finally available for study. In this setting he began his life's work. It eventually culminated in the *Summa Theologica*, that calm, rational study of the Christian faith as considered in the light of the philosophical revolution inspired by Aristotle's writings. This great work, along with his other textbooks, commentaries and lectures, is now considered the height of orthodoxy. When it was first written, violent controversies raged around it; books were burned at Oxford, and certain parts even banned by one outraged bishop.

Seven hundred years later, the dust has settled, the old antagonists are long gone and St. Thomas Aquinas is venerated as the patron of schools and universities. How appropriate! What better role model for students than one who once shocked his family, vociferously championed the new learning and dearly loved a good argument?

The Presentation

February 2

The ancient Mosaic laws, described in great and bewildering detail in such Old Testament books as Leviticus and Deuteronomy, set forth a code of behaviour regulating all aspects of life from birth to death. The rituals of clean and unclean foods, the sacrifices, acts of worship and annual feasts – all were established to set the Israelites apart from their neighbours and to commemorate the covenant into which they entered as God's chosen people.

We see this ancient Law being observed on this day in the life of the infant Jesus: the ritual purification of Mary after the birth of her child, and the dedication of Jesus, her first born, to the Lord. These special events took place in Jerusalem, the religious and political centre of Judaism and the only place of worship for the devout.*

These Jewish rituals of purification and dedication (or "presentation") were supposed to take place forty days after a boy's birth and, coming upon the event from our perspective today, we are able to appreciate the many echoes that resonate back and forth through the narrative. The "forty days" immediately calls to mind the forty days

* Recently, we have seen a shift in emphasis on this feast. Today we focus more on Jesus' religious initiation and less on Mary's ritual purification. This day was also known as "Candlemas" because candles, symbolizing Christ as the light of the gentiles, would be blessed today.

that Jesus was to stay in the desert at the beginning of his public life, praying and fasting, exposed to the temptations of Satan but ultimately successful in walking away from the lures of power, ambition and pride. We are likewise familiar with another period of forty days: the time between Christ's rising from the dead and his ascension into heaven, the beginning of a new life of witness for the apostles and of celebration for the Church throughout the ages. Again, in our own lives, we experience the forty days of Lent, a season of prayer and renewal in preparation for the new life of Easter.

These three observances, widely separated in time and purpose, are themselves echoes of the forty years that Moses and the Israelites spent wandering in the desert until they could enter the promised land. For them this was a time of trial, punishment and preparation, sustained by miracles and the presence of the Lord, but a time of testing nevertheless.

So much of our belief seems to involve these backward and forward echoes and images: events in the Old Testament which foreshadow the Gospels; descriptions in the New Testament which deliberately evoke earlier traditions and prophecies; conscious attempts throughout the centuries to mirror the events of Jesus' life in our ongoing day-to-day activities of liturgy, prayer and meditation.

The rich texture created by these many strands of tradition, revelations and observances, woven together from many sources over hundreds of years, has always served to bring forth the same message: the message of a God who loves us and cares about our welfare. It is no coincidence that this is the theme of the prophecies made by the aged Simeon and Anna when they see the baby boy brought by his parents to the Temple, in accordance with the ancient law: "Lord, your word has been fulfilled... my eyes have seen salvation."

Our Lady of Lourdes

February 11

The small town of Lourdes, set in the mountains of southwestern France in the *département* of the High Pyrenees, is blessed with dramatic natural beauty. The train trip south from Paris is an interesting beginning to our pilgrimage, as we pass through a variety of prosperous farmlands before climbing into the high rugged upland pastures and wooded slopes that will be our destination. Even the railway station off-season is pleasant; during the summer crush of travellers, it will be crowded and chaotic. The main street looks like it could be found in Banff, Aspen, or any other alpine playground catering to international tourists, with one subtle difference: closer to the holy sites are shop after shop selling religious souvenirs, some tasteful, many atrocious. This blend of sacred and secular is in turn surrounded by cheap restaurants, guest houses, one or two luxury hotels, and other establishments of the sort patronized by travellers everywhere.

In the evenings at Lourdes, everyone gathers in the silence of the grotto (the famous spot where the beautiful Lady had appeared to the young Bernadette back in

1858),[*] and after paying homage to the spring of living water that gushed forth as a sign at Our Lady's bequest, the faithful form a procession. We each receive a candle and, hundreds or thousands strong, the crowd prepares to walk through the grounds of the sanctuary saying the rosary and singing a few hymns. All standard stuff so far; however, to the praise and everlasting glory of Our Lord and his blessed mother, this rosary quickly becomes something much greater than just the monotonous recitation of familiar prayers. As we pass by the chapels and the gardens, we are led through our rosary by pilgrims from different lands, our decades of Hail Marys ringing forth in English, French, Spanish, Italian, Portuguese or German, with maybe Korean and other languages unfamiliar to the Western ear included. This multinational, multiracial prayer is interrupted only by the hymns, likewise sung in a dazzling tapestry of languages, reflecting another multitude of traditions. Soon people start to light their candles, passing the flame around to their neighbours. Darkness starts to fall as our long procession slowly snakes along the paths near the sanctuaries, our flickering candles, some carried in unsteady hands, forming a chain of stars in the gathering twilight.

Meanwhile, as the tribute to the Beautiful Lady continues, we slowly become more aware of those on the sidelines in their hospital beds and wheelchairs, the disabled,

* There are many recorded apparitions of the Blessed Virgin besides this one, including other famous ones at Fatima, Portugal, and Guadalupe, Mexico. Interestingly enough, most of these apparitions have been to women and children. At the present time, a series of supernatural experiences by some young people in Medjugorje, Yugoslavia, are under examination.

the paralysed, those beyond the reach of science who come to the waters in hope of a cure, joining as best they can in the prayers and songs. And so our procession continues, this assembly of visitors from every land, young and old, rich and poor, healthy and sick, becoming a living witness to the pilgrim Church on earth, all joined together singing and praying in the gathering dusk, "Ave, Ave, Ave Maria."*

* "Immaculate Mary," popular in many Catholic grade schools, is the traditional Lourdes hymn.

Shrove Tuesday

Shrove Tuesday doesn't pack the punch today that it once did in years gone by. When fasting meant real hunger and not "light sensible eating"; when meatless days meant lentil soup and not pasta salad; when social activities ground to a halt and even weddings were forbidden – in those far-off centuries, the day before Lent started was the last chance to have a decent meal, make a little noise and carouse with one's neighbours for several weeks.

The Mardi Gras parades in New Orleans, the Carnival in Rio and, on a lesser scale, the *carnevales** enjoyed in many Latin countries, are the remnants of that tradition, perhaps robbed today of their religious significance but no less fun for all those who enjoy display, whether spontaneous or contrived, and a little unbridled hedonism for a day or two. Surely everyone has a secret fantasy of dancing down the streets of some exotic foreign city on a warm winter night with dozens of other outrageously dressed and uninhibited revellers!

And just what are we left with in the damp and chilly gloom of a northern winter? Not throbbing drums pulsing to some jungle rhythm; not even a few good-natured town

---

* *Mardi gras* in French means "fat Tuesday," referring to the luxuries of the table enjoyed on this day before the austerities of Lent would begin. *Carnevale* in Latin languages reminds us that there would be much abstaining from meat during Lent: *carne* = meat, *vale* = go.

musicians entertaining us with accordion and fiddle. No plumed and sequined Bird of Paradise could be tempted to samba down our salt-stained streets, no matter how mild the winter. No, my friends, we are left with pancakes,* not hedonism, not exotic fruits, not wild dances, and barely enough public consciousness to organize a few pancake lunches in the grade schools.

In days of yore, the pancakes were supposed to use up all the eggs hanging around the kitchen before Lent started, the better to ensure a strict vegetarian approach to dinner for the next forty days. "Shrove," it seems, comes from the word "to confess," though it's hard to know whether this means that people made a lenten confession in anticipation of a holy and pious season or in repentance after a particularly wild and successful Mardi Gras.

One family may serve their homemade flapjacks with blueberry sauce, sour cream and a grilled breakfast sausage or two on the side. Another may set out thin crepes to be rolled with lemon, sugar and jam. Yet a third will experiment with pancakes stuffed with apples and cinnamon. Admirable, enjoyable meals these may be, but a long way removed from those heady Latin rhythms and bodies swaying down the street, the roast suckling pigs and the strong wines of yesteryear. Ah, progress.

---

* The *Oxford English Dictionary* records the first use of "Shrove Tuesday" in 1500. By 1615, one T. Herbert was using the phrase "as flat as a Shrove Tuesday pancake."

Ash Wednesday

Some folks might think that Ash Wednesday would be a sombre day, harkening back to Mediaeval times when penance was really penance, ushering in the biblical forty days* of austerity, mortification and general doom and gloom. The language that we hear in our services today reinforces the sobriety and general seriousness of purpose appropriate to the beginning of a penitential season: "remember thou art dust and unto dust thou shalt return." Some congregations may hear a slightly less bleak formula in these enlightened times, but the message is the same. However much we may try to stave off the evil day, we are all going to die, each and every one of us. No amount of clean living, fitness testing, vitamin therapy or wishful thinking will deflect this our ultimate fate. It is a sobering, perhaps unwelcome thought, and we all need to be reminded of it once in a while.

But Ash Wednesday does not appear to be an unpopular or unpleasant day. The churches are packed, hordes of people regularly turning out: at early morning services before work; in the downtown parishes at lunch time; at school masses during the day; for family services in the

* Ash Wednesday was established as the first day of Lent back in the late sixth century by Pope St. Gregory the Great, the last of the Fathers of the Church. The forty days do not include the six Sundays which fall between Ash Wednesday and Easter.

evening after supper. There is something stirring, even awe-inspiring, about this centuries-old ritual taking place on an ordinary workday, as we all become collectively more aware of our own finite limitations. In a society for which death and decay have become the only obscenities left, how strange it is for us to seek out with such enthusiasm this opportunity to remember our own mortality!

And yet, while none of us relishes the idea of greeting Sister Death, as Francis of Assisi might say, we are far from averse to the experience we share with each other on Ash Wednesday. We may even enjoy being singled out for a little while, our foreheads smudged and dirty, feeling righteous and conspicuous like old-time witnesses for religion. Children, and those child-like in their appreciation of these little rituals of life, always hope for "lots of ashes,"* the better to make this once-a-year statement of faith.

As we leave the church after our annual reminder of the way of all flesh, we are left with a feeling of hope, not gloom, of patience, not depression. After being at this mass, we always feel if anything a little more alive, with a definite and good reason for walking out into the world, ashes and all, going in peace to love and serve the Lord for as long as he cares to spare us.

---

* The leftover palms from the previous year's Palm Sunday are burned to make the ashes used today. In biblical times, ashes were frequently rubbed on the head and face as a sign of mourning and penance, the origin of the phrase "sackcloth and ashes."

First Sunday in Lent

We have moved a long way from the austere concepts of prayer and fasting that marked the early experiences of Lent. No one uses expressions such as "mortifying the flesh" much these days. Nevertheless, lenten observances are far from dead, even in these supposedly decadent times. Some people do indeed give things up as they did in the past.

One grandmother with a sweet tooth swears off all desserts, a real hardship for her; another goes without butter. One Greek Orthodox woman abstains from red meat, and since her husband doesn't join her, there needs to be lots of extra cooking and meal planning in their household, a form of penance for sure. An older gentleman, a first-class athlete and bon vivant, cuts out all alcohol. A prominent Anglican doctor tries to live without chocolate. Some people resurrect the meatless Wednesday and Friday* routine and hope they will like fish when it's on the menu for dinner.

---

* In ancient times, Mondays and Thursdays were fast days for devout Jews; Wednesdays and Fridays in turn became the traditional penitential days in Christianity. Wednesday was chosen because it is a tradition that Judas betrayed Our Lord on this day. We have customarily regarded Friday as the day of the Crucifixion, although there is no real scriptural agreement on its date. John's gospel places the Last Supper on a Wednesday; the other three evangelists on a Thursday.

Lots of other beneficial lenten practices keep cropping up: the mother of four who reads the New Testament; another who starts in on Genesis and tries to keep going. Attendance at weekday mass increases; the parish organizes its ShareLife campaign; donations start coming in. Explaining all these positive aspects of Lent to our non-believing friends is easy enough; the "prayer and almsgiving" side is within most people's understanding. But how can an educated, supposedly sophisticated, modern mind possibly make sense of the childish restrictions grouped together under the umbrella of "giving up"?

Perhaps acting like a child once in a while is not so foolish, even if it means participating in these supposedly outdated traditions. For one thing, arbitrary petty restrictions are great ways to heighten our awareness and understanding of a season that requires more introspective thought than, say, Christmastime or summer holidays. At first our unconscious mind wants to "forget" about our little resolutions and "absent-mindedly" we may reach for that candy bar or glass of wine. When we pull ourselves back, however, ignoring all the old-fashioned sermons about disciplining the will and conquering our passions, we are really reminding ourselves that not every day in our year is the same. Remembering to be festive is easy enough. No one wakes up on Christmas morning and "absent-mindedly" gets dressed for work. But how many of us turn naturally to the spirit of quiet and thoughtfulness that should mark the days before Good Friday?

It is a refreshing change for us to give ourselves permission to dwell somewhere else for a very little while every year, where we can shake ourselves free from a few of our regular habits. Habits, not vices – there's nothing wrong with chocolate mousse, however much the food editors love to use the word "sinful." By "giving things up" we recognize the changing seasons on our liturgical calendar, and we allow ourselves to savour the well-deserved contrast between the days of celebration waiting for us at Easter and the days of preparation that belong to Lent.

St. Patrick's Day

March 17

Once a year in North America, our attention is turned to Ireland, not as a source of headlines on terrorist bombings, but in an entirely light-hearted diversion at the end of winter. Shamrocks, green beer, leprechauns, the blarney stone – these touchstones of the popular image of the Emerald Isle are all trotted out. There is much wearing o'the green; "Danny Boy" and "When Irish Eyes are Smiling" can be heard on the radio; classical stations bring out the John McCormack recordings.

In schools, the situation is much the same. More popular legends, religious this time, are told: St. Patrick and the shamrock, St. Patrick and the snakes. Taken all in all, there is not much here, in the secular or religious tradition, to justify all the fuss. Nevertheless, a very little research into the background of Celtic Christianity reveals a wealth of interesting and inspiring material that deserves to be more widely known.

So, putting aside the funny greeting cards and the shamrock-shaped cookies, let us instead turn our imaginations to a wild and very distant land about fifteen hundred years ago, to an island well beyond the sophisticated urban centres civilized by Roman rule. We can imagine a land of great natural beauty, rocky and remote, with windy shores and breathtaking headlands, not even vaguely similar to the lush Mediterranean vineyards, prosperous farms and gracious villas that would be familiar to the Pope and his bishops suddenly interested in this barbaric northern country "with no towns."

Patrick, a Roman citizen living in Britain, appears in this semi-pagan landscape, but not as the very first missionary, as popular lore would have it. A respectable number of Christians, most with unfamiliar names, had already preceded him, complete with legends of miraculous activities and intense religious fervour. When Patrick (a very real person, however little we may know about him with any certainty) does arrive, his great gifts and virtues enable him to consolidate the work of these forerunners, St. Declan being the easiest to pronounce. Later biographers created the fanciful but inspiring histories of Patrick, perhaps in an attempt to explain the immense explosion that is soon to become Celtic Christianity.*

In the next centuries we can witness a flowering of activity that nearly overwhelms us: the splendid life of the intensely beloved St. Brigid, called the "Mary of the Gael"; the miraculous wanderings of St. Brendan in his fragile skin boat, perhaps even his landfall in North America; the austere isolation of the monks clinging to a solitary existence on the rugged offshore islands; the artistic tradition that created splendid illuminated manuscripts such as *The Book of Kells;* the missionary activities of

* In ages past, many books were written with the sincere purpose of edifying their readers; in some of these works, there may also have been an unscientific disregard for what we now call historical fact.

others like Colm and Columban who kept learning alive while the rest of Europe was still in the dark ages.

All of these and the many other achievements of later generations merit our respect and attention on March 17, the day dedicated to the patron saint of Ireland. In looking for the source of much that is wonderful in the Irish Christian heritage, we have efficiently wrapped up all sorts of shadowy fourth- and fifth-century holy men and women under the aegis* of "St. Patrick." History will never be able to tell us how much or how little he may actually have done; nevertheless, we are all greatly in debt to the culture that produced the poets, teachers, musicians, scholars, artists and mystics who followed in his wake, to enrich our world beyond measure.

---

* In ancient mythology, the aegis was a shield or protective armour used by the gods. By extension, we use this word today to refer to the protection and influence that one person can extend over others. Continuing this image is the beautiful prayer, "St. Patrick's Breastplate," with its stirring description of Christ as our shield against all the woes of the world.

The Vernal Equinox

March 21

The coming of spring means different things to different people. For the mothers of toddlers and school-age youngsters, it marks the end of the season of snowsuits, leaky boots, lost mittens, wet scarves and runny noses, and it ushers in a season of mud, dirty sneakers, scraped knees and lost umbrellas. For the elderly confined to small apartments, it may mean release from the bondage created by dangerous sidewalks, treacherous steps and icy driveways. In the countryside, farmers look forward to working in their fields again and caring for newborn livestock; in the cities those close to the land are happy to help their gardens come back to life. Up in the north, there is still lots more winter to endure, but at least the days are appreciably longer, the very bitter cold is over, and the sun is starting to get stronger. For all of us in Canada, winter, for all its austere beauty and its exhilarating briskness, can be a trial at times, no matter how positive our outlook and how enthusiastic we are about snow.

With the official arrival of spring, regardless of the actual weather, we seem to be collectively acknowledging the time of growth and regeneration, all part of the universal cycle of death and rebirth. The popular images associated with this season – newborn lambs, baby animals of all kinds, the first flowers – all draw on the normal phenomena common to the natural world and, whether we live in the country or the city, we find these images appealing and powerful. Even our clothing reflects this delight in spring as we hurry to shed our drab winter coats, our woollen turtlenecks and our heavy socks, and pull out the pastel shirts, cotton sweaters and flowered dresses, in happy anticipation of the warm days and short nights that are just around the corner.

All this involvement with new growth and celebration is very aptly timed in our liturgical calendars. To paraphrase the poet, "If Spring comes, can Easter be far behind?" * As we all learned once upon a time, Easter is one of our moveable feasts, and indeed its date is intimately linked to the coming of spring. For Easter comes on the first Sunday after the first full moon after the vernal equinox,** the better to light the way of pilgrims everywhere.

---

* Percy Bysshe Shelley (1792-1822) from "Ode to the West Wind"–"If Winter comes, can Spring be far behind?"

** The vernal (for spring) and autumnal (for fall) equinoxes are the only times in the year when day and night are exactly "equal" in length. This way of calculating the date of Easter was fixed at the council of Nicea in 325 A. D.

The Annunciation

March 25

Sometime in the penitential season of Lent, we are allowed to take a short holiday and skip ahead nine months in our imagination to December 25. Sarcastic radio announcers may groan "275 shopping days until Christmas," but we will disregard them. March 25 was the first of the four "quarter days"* that used to mark off the year, the traditional times for paying and receiving rents, discharging debts and transacting all sorts of financial business. The feast of the Annunciation was once known as "Lady Day," a name that evokes all the homage, chivalry and old-fashioned respect paid to Mary throughout the ages. This feast has remained one of the most beautiful and inspiring in the salvation tradition that has formed our faith for two thousand years.

Dozens of Renaissance painters used the theme of the Annunciation for some of their finest works, and art books are full of the graceful angels and submissive virgins that came forth from all those talented brushes. In turn, enough Christmas cards and reproductions of these famous works have been sold to make the story as familiar to us as Christmas itself. Each time we say a "Hail Mary," we recall the angel Gabriel's greeting: "Hail, full of grace,

* The other quarter days are June 24 (midsummer), September 29 (Michaelmas) and December 25 (Christmas).

the Lord is with you." Mary's answer, "Behold the handmaid of the Lord," in its charming old-fashioned form, may not be as immediately familiar to us unless we remember the Angelus* from days gone by. But beyond the commonplace and the obscure, the meaning of this feast is never in any doubt, for it is captured in just one word: Yes!

The role that Mary is asked to play in the great drama that we watch and witness throughout the year combines all the maternal tenderness, strength of purpose, self-sacrifice and tragic loss of the greatest fictional heroine. But Mary enters the stage in all simplicity and has only one thing to say when presented with this earth-shattering challenge: "Let what you have said be done to me." Her single-minded acceptance of God's will, as described in the beginning of Luke's gospel, is the greatest difference between her life and our own. All the rest of us, at one time or another, hear a call but don't listen; see the path but don't follow; put down our burdens, ignore our responsibilities, shirk our duties and just plain wander off the road of salvation.

Mary did not know the exact way in which she would find herself being "God's handmaiden." Whatever joy,

---

* In Catholic communities in the "old days," the church bells would ring out to mark the Angelus, morning, noon and night. Labourers in the fields and others at work would stop to say this prayer which recounts the story of the Annunciation:

> The Angel of the Lord declared unto Mary
> And she conceived of the Holy Spirit.
> "Behold the handmaid of the Lord,
> Be it done unto me according to thy Word."
> And the Word was made flesh,
> And dwelt among us.

excitement and anticipation she may have felt about her son who would be great, the Son of the Most High, complete with throne and a reign that would never end, she could have had no inkling of all that would accompany that promise. She could not see the cross or the tomb, the pain or the suffering that no mother can bear to imagine for her children. In the middle of Lent, hundreds of years later, we know about these things; we have had a peek at the end of the story. Our own destinies, however, are just as hidden from us as Mary's was to her on that fine day when Gabriel came down with the momentous news, wings shimmering and draperies billowing in the heavenly wind. May the Lord grant that we can accept the challenges of our future with the same peace and graciousness that Mary did.

Third World Solidarity Day

Fifth Sunday of Lent

In the good old days, we used to have Mission Sunday,* and maybe some grizzled, sunburned veteran of life in an African or South American outpost would come by to preach a sermon. Sometimes these good fathers would merely string together a series of anecdotes for the entertainment and edification of the parish audience, touching on their work, the heat, the disease and the dirt, the better to stimulate generosity for the second collections to be held after Communion for the "missions." School children were always saving stamps, collecting old eyeglasses, praying for lepers, holding raffles and, once in a while, even worrying about the teeming millions out there.

Today, we talk about the "third world"** and we are able to discuss its problems with greater socio-economic sophistication. We know a great deal more about the history and geography of these "mission countries"; sometimes we even visit them, now that tourism is a worldwide business. Nevertheless we often close our eyes to the bond that links us all together in one universal human family.

How many of us ever bother to think about those far-off "teeming millions," not as projects or statistics or worthwhile causes, but as people, just like you and me?

---

* The third Sunday in October is now known as World Mission Day.

** This term refers to the developing nations of Asia, Africa and Latin America.

Would we be uncomfortable, unnerved or embarrassed to find ourselves suddenly surrounded by a sea of brown, black, yellow or red faces? If language were no barrier, would we have anything to say?

The third world is not just an issue for group discussion, but a daily presence, one that is coming closer to all our lives. Standing on a Toronto subway platform each day we see new arrivals from every corner of the map. Northern and western Canadian towns are finally coming to terms with their own large "indigenous populations." The voices coming out of some radio and television sets are often not speaking any recognizable language. There is even a trend towards multiracial music that combines Caribbean, African and other non-Western traditions into a tasty cross-cultural stew. Racially mixed couples are more common these days. The face of our world has indeed changed.

In spite of the many encouraging advances, problems continue: racism in schools; unfair hiring practices; inequalities in the justice system; growing numbers of homeless people on our own city streets. The only hope for a permanent solution is the whole-hearted recognition of the dignity and value of every human being – here and in the Third World – simple as that may sound. We are all used to hearing the phrase, "brothers and sisters in Christ." It is easy enough to acknowledge those who are well fed, attractively dressed and easy to understand. Oh Lord, help us to love all the guests you have invited to your table.

Passion (Palm) Sunday

Sixth Sunday of Lent

Of all the Sundays in the year, this is the one most devoted to irony, the startling contrast between what we expect and what actually occurs, a device beloved of dramatists everywhere but not exactly something we normally find in a church.

On this day we commemorate Jesus' triumphal entry into Jerusalem as crowds of the faithful lined his way, shouting "*hosanna*"* and waving palm fronds in his honour. Today in memory of that event, we eagerly raise our fresh tropical greenery while the priest blesses us, and we remember the words of that long-ago procession, "Blessed is he who comes in the name of the Lord."

After recalling this splendid public affirmation of love and faith on the part of Jesus' followers, we immediately move on to the full-scale reading of the events of his last days, where we see the very same crowd of people turned into a vengeful mob, not content with palms and hosannas, but armed with cruel mocking taunts and insults. A few short days after the events in Scene I, the hosannas have given way to shouts of "Give us Barrabas!" With exquisite cruelty, the crowds find a new voice to comment on his suffering: "He saved others, let him save himself."

---

* *Hosanna* is a Hebrew word meaning, "O Lord, save, we pray." We also use it in the mass at the Sanctus when we say, "Hosanna in the highest."

And so the gospel story unfolds, ending as we know with the death and burial of Jesus. The worshippers in our churches listen respectfully; the mass continues and is eventually over. The faithful return home with little pieces of this year's palm to braid around a picture frame in a bedroom; to weave into a cross and hang over a doorway; to tie around the arm of a stone angel in the cemetery. And the irony continues. Do we accord the holy palm this reverence because it evokes the scene of that blessed entry into Jerusalem so long ago? Or unconsciously do we cherish these slim green branches because they remind us that we are just as fickle as the crowds chanting "Peace in heaven" one day and "Crucify him" the next?

Holy Thursday

The liturgy in which we now participate on Holy Thursday evenings is not one which some of us remember sentimentally from bygone days. As part of the reformed Holy Week liturgy re-introduced to modern Catholics in the last few decades, this very moving, sometimes surprising commemoration of the events of the Last Supper has only recently become popular in our house.

Back in the 1950s on Holy Thursday night, our family instead continued an age-old custom by visiting seven churches on our own private pilgrimage. The whole family piled into the car and off we went, to have a first-hand experience of the city's multi-cultural fabric as we sampled the widest variety of ethnic churches we could manage. Crisscrossing the downtown streets, we would try to include St. Stanislaus, the tiny semi-circular Polish church with beautifully carved old wooden pews; St. Patrick's, a German parish with wonderful singing; St. Mary's, near our father's old stomping grounds, today serving the Portuguese community; St. Basil's, on the campus of the University, stately and dignified; Mount Carmel, home to the first Italian immigrants at the turn of the century and now in the middle of Chinatown. We would visit our regular parish close to home only if imagination or the weather failed. Lumbering along, six or seven in the car, listening to the hockey game between stops, we loved this exploration of foreign territory, marvelled at the elaborate decorations prepared for the repository altars, and enjoyed our own family fellowship for a few hours.

Wonderful as those Holy Thursday pilgrimages were (and they were one of the family's favourite events of the year!), the new liturgy celebrated these days provides stiff competition for our fondest memories. Today's service begins with a special entrance procession into the church, warning even the most casual observer that something important is about to happen – all the clergy the parish can muster, several lay readers, altar servers galore, plus eucharistic ministers and representatives of the congregation – a very satisfying, democratic spectacle indeed. The long mass gets under way; the congregation always seems to sing the "Gloria" with special enthusiasm after forty days of lenten abstinence. The sacred scriptures remind us of the various events we are commemorating on this evening: the Passover story from Exodus, a Passover that Jesus himself was planning to celebrate in Jerusalem in time-honoured Jewish tradition; then Paul's simple, unadorned description for his friends of the events of the Last Supper, events which we in turn remember each and every time we go to mass; and finally, the passage in John's gospel where Jesus, the Lord and Master, acts as a servant and washes the dust from the feet of his astonished disciples.

There is lots more too, not least of which is the procession at the very end as the blessed sacrament is carried around the church. In some lucky parishes, the great chant melody, "Pange Lingua," is sung, verse after verse linking our worship today with a musical tradition over a thousand years old.

And speaking of traditions, some time-honoured customs associated with our faith fade away and we may sorely miss them. New ones may or may not come on the scene to take their places.* That seems to be part of life. Our road is much easier to follow if we accept that behind all this change, adaptation and innovation is a sincere struggle to find the very best way to obey that simple commandment: "Do this in memory of me."

* The former name for this great day was "Maundy Thursday"; it is still used in many Protestant churches. "Maundy," an unusual and little understood word, recalls the Latin verb *mandare*, to command, in remembrance of Jesus' commands to his apostles as recorded in the Gospels. Almsgiving and gifts were also included in the ancient festivals.

Good Friday

Steadfast Cross, amongst all others
Thou art a tree most to prize;
In branch and flower, such another
I know not one in wood or rise.
Sweet be the nails and sweet be the tree
And sweeter be the burden that hangs on thee.[*]

The cross as a symbol, both sacred and secular, is familiar to everyone in our society. This central image of Christianity is all around us: there is the Red Cross, international non-denominational symbol for "help"; the crosses of St. George, St. Andrew and St. Patrick[**] find their way onto flags flying all around the world; even the exotic Alfa Romeo sports cars include a cross on their official logo, as part of the age-old emblem of the municipality of Milan. A quick trip to the reference library also reminds us that the "cross is an ancient symbol of many uses" familiar in Carthaginian designs, Scandinavian

[*] This little poem is a slightly updated version of a fourteenth-century lyric, itself a mediaeval interpretation of the long sixth-century masterpiece, "Pange Lingua," or "Sing, My Tongue." A more modern translation is used today at the Veneration of the Cross. This hymn derives from the Gallican rite of ancient France.

[**] The Union Jack combines the crosses of Saints George, Andrew and Patrick, representing the lands of England, Scotland and Ireland. There are numerous designs for the Cross, including the familiar Latin cross; the Greek cross with its arms of equal length; the Anchor cross used by the early Christians in the catacombs; the Tau cross in the shape of a capital T, and so on.

runes, Roman astronomies, ancient Egyptian tombs, pre-Colombian Aztec sites and God-knows-what-else.

But regardless of the prevalence of this simple but evocative emblem in many different cultures, the Christian understanding of the cross is unique, complex and paradoxical. This most essential symbol of the events in our faith has never been easy to understand or accept, but we all seem to agree that whatever else we may dispute in the teachings and traditions of the Church, and however we may feel out of touch with this or any other generation of belief, there once was a man and he died.

And we hardly need to be reminded that we can, even today and through our faith, enter into the suffering of Jesus on that first Good Friday, for, as another popular expression puts it, "we each have our cross to bear." There seems no end to the suffering that humanity is undergoing on any given day, and the mass media are ever ready to exploit all the various and unhappy events taking place somewhere around the world. But even if we had complete indifference to the plight of others, each one of us, no matter how privileged, has experienced pain, illness, disappointment and fear, and at the end of each life, however long or short, rich or poor, there will be a grave waiting too.

Many a sensitive soul has been overwhelmed by the ongoing prospect of so much pain, whether personal or cosmic, but in faith we can receive far more than superficial consolation from our consideration of Jesus' life and death. The Good News of Easter is bound up in the events of Good Friday; there can be no resurrection unless there is also a burial. Learned theologians may have struggled for generations to describe the true meaning of Jesus' death on the cross. They will continue to wrestle with this question of salvation, appropriately enough described in the mass as the "mystery of faith," for the cross is at the centre of the Christian message. Good Friday is the day on which we set aside all our legitimate concerns and uncertainties, all our doubts and arguments, to join with believers of every time and place in that humble but infinitely evocative prayer: "Lord, by your cross and resurrection you have set us free."

Easter Vigil

In ancient Greek mythology, Prometheus stole fire from the gods and brought it down to those on earth. For his crime, he was imprisoned on a rock to which an eagle came by day to tear out his liver; every night the liver would grow back again. Somehow, Prometheus was eventually freed from this bizarre and never-ending punishment, but the moral of his story was clear: in the pagan world, gods and humans were engaged in an eternal rivalry with each other and lived out the struggle in a series of episodes marked by heroism, treachery, jealousy and fierceness.

This old Greek story is still entertaining and has served to inspire assorted works of genius from poets and artists drawn to a myth, however fanciful, about the origin of fire. More scientifically, archaeologists and anthropologists have much to say about the role that fire played in the process of our evolution. Where would we be now without fire, used from prehistoric times to bring warmth, to cook food, to protect the community, eventually in the first tentative struggles to make a brutal life easier, to create what we now call technology?

And if fire is the magic weapon that we could use to subdue the hostile animal kingdom lurking outside in the darkness, speech is the first accomplishment that would allow us to share more than mere food and warmth with those of our own kind huddled together around those prehistoric campsites.

The rituals of our Easter Vigil* involve both of these ancient touchstones of human development, first of all with the lighting of the new fire, dramatically accomplished in the pitch dark church, drawing on our most primitive hopes and fears. This is followed by a lengthy liturgy of the Word, a tribute to human speech, refined and developed into writing and literature in order to share the history of our thoughts and dreams with our neighbours, over thousands of years of time and uncounted miles of space.

And there's more – after these two timeless fundamentals, we then add the blessing of the Easter Water, for water is the most basic need of all living creatures. We can survive for a long time without food; we last only a few days without water.

Indeed we can go through life without the Light of the World, the Word-made-flesh, or the Living Water, but as seekers of spiritual understanding have always known, we would not be fully alive. And we are thankful on this spring evening to have reached enough of that understanding to be here together in this church, greeting the risen Christ in our hearts and in our lives.

---

* It has been a tradition to honour a very great feast not just on the day of its celebration but also on the night before, its "vigil," as we wait and pray for the wonderful day to come. St. Augustine called this evening the "mother of all vigils," recognizing the supreme importance of Easter in the liturgical calendar. Furthermore, the liturgical day officially begins at 4:00 p.m., "sundown," a custom taken over from Judaism. We also remember this observance in our midnight masses on Christmas Eve.

Easter Sunday

A large extended family, complete with grandparents, cousins and in-laws, gathers in a North Toronto house for brunch on Easter Sunday. The noon hour time is carefully chosen so that several of the married children can leave early for another set of visits to more relatives in Hamilton and Scarborough. And the cooking has been divided up so that no one household is unduly disrupted by the holiday preparations.

The menu has also come under severe scrutiny – not too rich in consideration of those who are having a couple of celebrations that day; not too exotic so that the children can enjoy themselves also. There is ham, this family's traditional counterpoint to the Christmas turkey; salads, a tribute to the good weather that is just around the corner; eggs, an ancient dish that symbolizes the Easter message of new life. There are also a few traditional sweets updated for the modern table. The Colomba, an Italian Easter bread in the shape of a dove, has a luscious chocolate coating. The customary cheesecake sports a wild blueberry sauce this year. And for children of all ages, there is a basket of marshmallow and candy bunnies.*

Conversation is lively at the two tables set up to accommodate the large group: one couple describes the Easter Vigil service in their new parish the night before, a marathon that included five baptisms. Another aunt has a nephew deep in conversation over his high school English program. All in all, nothing could be nicer than this happy informal get-together, arranged judiciously and tactfully to please everyone.

And yet every person at the table has also brought a burden of personal cares along for the celebrations. Several guests have had serious health problems and saw the inside of more than one hospital during the year. One or two have had a few anxious moments contemplating their bank statements. Not every child has had a wonderful, successful time at school. There are even a few family members conspicuous by their absence, involved in projects that can't be shared, even on Easter. And the conversation finally turns to the relatives now departed, some after rich and happy lives, some in youthful tragedy, still remembered and mourned.

But by some miracle, the atmosphere of celebration clearly outshines any other consideration, for a few hours at least. Business problems, the hassles of growing up, our own frail mortality – all these are forgotten, and peace and

* Many European cultures have been far more interested in Easter than in Christmas as a time of secular and family celebration. Roast or stewed lamb is also popularly associated with Easter menus, especially in Mediterranean countries.

harmony reign instead. It seems we have been living part of the Easter message: "Whenever two or more of you are gathered together in my name, there I am in the midst of you."

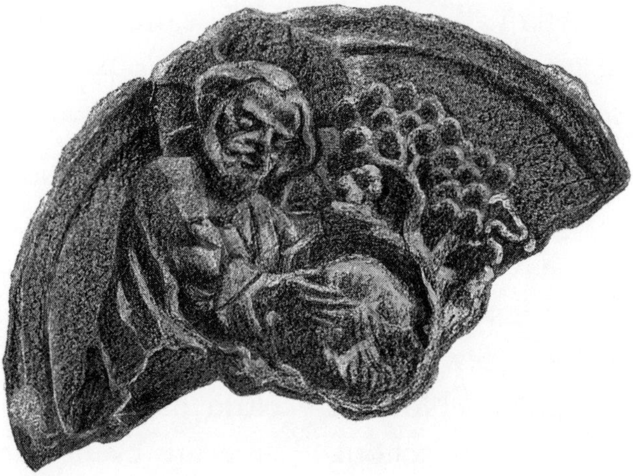

St. Catherine of Siena

1347-1380

April 29

In 1347, the dreaded Black Death began one of its periodic marches of devastation across Europe. Nearly one third of the population was wiped out by a plague that had no apparent cause or cure. The Hundred Years' War, meanwhile, had been wreaking its own havoc on the poor folks of France and England for ten years by then. Political conditions in Italy, exclusive of the destruction caused by the Black Death, had been chaotic for generations. The papacy, including the extensive administrative and financial branches, had deserted the turbulence of Rome for the relative safety of Avignon* in the south of France. Ongoing struggles between rival factions of the rapacious nobles had kept central Italy in an unsettled condition for decades. In the north, the Ghibellines and Guelphs had been engaged in another futile series of civil disturbances, petty wars that ended up costing half the Church's revenues.

Into this unhappy century, Catherine Benincasa was born in Siena in 1347. Hardly a day goes by when we are

* The popes lived in Avignon for nearly seventy years; this unfortunate period was referred to poetically as the "Babylonian Captivity," in remembrance of the exile of the Jews to Babylon after the fall of Jerusalem from 586 B.C. to 538 B.C.

not made aware of the turmoil of our own world, thanks to our ever efficient mass media. When Catherine experienced her first visions at the age of seven, however, she was completely ignorant of the affairs that convulsed all Europe. Yet something was to lead her out of her father's humble home and onto the world stage in a personal involvement with some of the major crises of the mid-fourteenth century.

Catherine was the uneducated daughter of a workman, yet she became a Dominican tertiary,* the advisor of the Pope and a great traveller, one of the more unlikely scenarios in world history. How did she do this? Her life is a study in contrasts. On the one hand we have the records of her mystical experiences as documented in her book, *The Dialogue*. In art, she is often depicted with a ring, symbolizing her mystical marriage to Christ, or with the stigmata.** On the other hand, there are her hundreds of letters, all aimed at a public far removed from the isolated cell of a mystic. She travelled, in the days when a trip of one hundred miles was an almost unthinkable excursion for a peasant. From Siena to Avignon, Florence, Rome and Pisa, she was involved in a multitude of activities. A crusade against the Turks, the return of the Pope from Avignon to Rome, the reorganization of the Church, the problem of the supporters of

---

* Many of the great religious orders of men and women also have tertiaries – Third Orders – lay people living in the world but associated with many of the goals and ideals of these religious institutes.

** The stigmata are the marks of the wounds of Christ that appear on some who have had extreme mystical experiences. These rare occurrences, more common in women than in men, are difficult to verify scientifically.

the anti-pope* – to these and other pressing and complex concerns she turned her energy and attention.

At first she worked on her own initiative; perhaps she interfered in areas that were theoretically of no concern to her. Eventually her participation was requested by those in charge, her enthusiasm and commitment eventually recognized as a great and rare gift. The combination of the contemplative life of asceticism and holiness with an active ministry involving diplomacy, foreign policy and international relations is an accomplishment seldom seen. In Catherine of Siena's case, these unique talents have been officially acknowledged for she was named a Doctor of the Church in 1970, only the second woman to receive this honour.

* To add to the chaos, at one point there were three popes, one legitimate and two false claimants or "anti-popes." There have been problems with anti-popes since the earliest days of the Fathers of the Church.

St. Joseph the Worker

May 1*

Writers of certain types of magazine articles never talk about work. The word is "career." "Career" implies glamour, wealth, mobility, promotion, creativity, satisfaction. "Work," on the other hand, carries with it more than a suggestion of old-fashioned boredom, starvation wages, monotony and stagnation. There is quite a difference between these two ways of spending the day from nine to five.

A wise doctor once remarked that both work and love are natural activities of the healthy human body. Nevertheless, most of us take jobs primarily from economic necessity, and it seems that our bodies may first need to adapt to purposeful activity before work can become "normal" for us. Another well-respected social commentator goes so far as to suggest that original sin is just another name for laziness. In that case, it is easy to see the reason why careers have always been so much more desirable than jobs.

Somehow or other, we have evolved a hierarchy of labour. It has varied from age to age: our high-priced doctors today may be embarrassed to remember that their

---

* May 1 is also the day celebrated in communist and socialist societies in honour of the workers of the world.

honoured profession was once considered little better than a barber's; today's wildly popular actors used to be in the same class as thieves. There was no "pink collar" ghetto in the Middle Ages: clerks and secretaries in those days were highly educated, well-paid men. But whatever our sliding scale for rating ourselves and our more or less fortunate neighbours, we do have the distressing habit of confusing a person's worth with his or her job.

When we cast an eye back over the variety of people singled out in many of the gospel stories, taking in Jesus' chosen friends and companions, we notice that few of them had "good jobs." Granted there were no stockbrokers or systems analysts or account executives to be had anywhere in Galilee, nor had the term "management professional" yet been invented. But it is an inescapable fact that Jesus chose to associate with people who worked, and not in upwardly mobile career opportunities either. Joseph we know as a carpenter,* not an interior design specialist. Matthew was a tax collector, Luke one of those low-status physicians, Simon Peter and his brother Andrew were fishermen. A few years later when Paul comes into the picture, we see him still earning a living as a tentmaker while he preaches the gospel around the Mediterranean.

Along with this collection of blue collar disciples, Jesus was also notorious for eating with prostitutes; talk-

* It has been suggested that St. Joseph trained Jesus as a carpenter and that, before the beginning of his public ministry, Jesus spent the hidden years in Nazareth working at this trade alongside his earthly father.

ing to adulterous women* (not something a respectable Jew would ever do); using the hated Samaritans as heroes in his parables; and conversing with lepers, the possessed, the blind and the lame. With a shock we realize that many of the familiar characters wandering through the gospels would be described as "street people" today!

Most of us no longer struggle at manual tasks; we sit at desks, not looms or spinning wheels; we move numbers, not bales of hay; we are inside more than out. We face different problems and challenges than the fishermen, shepherds, stewards and publicans of the gospel stories. But whether our job description says computer programmer, taxi driver, French teacher, store clerk, chambermaid, busboy, or lawyer, whether we work in a glamorous career or an underappreciated job, the words of the gospels still apply: "Come to me all you who labour and are burdened and I will refresh you."

* The longest recorded conversation in the gospels is between Jesus and the woman at the well. Jesus and his disciples also seem to have relied on their women followers for support while they were on the road.

World Day of Prayer for Vocations

No one in North America needs to be reminded of the shrinking numbers of our young people drawn to the religious life these days. Nor is this the place to examine the problem of the many others who, after a fair trial, are reluctantly obliged to admit they are unable to continue with their original vows. Nevertheless, even if these are bleak times for organized religion in general, there are yet a few families who have a special understanding of the word "vocation": mothers, fathers and siblings who have heard that one of their number thinks he or she might have a calling to the religious life.

Some of us hear the word *vocation*, and it sounds like a dreadful illness or a delusion, perhaps just one more dead-end avenue for a young person seemingly unable to settle down. Some families have been prepared for this choice by years of discussion and anticipation; for others, the announcement is a bolt out of the blue. When the news eventually starts to leak out to family and friends, reactions are mixed at best and there may be unseemly jokes about sex, money or job security, probably inspired as much by fear and ignorance as true mockery. Eventually the idea of this strange calling starts to be more familiar to everyone: there are lots of discussions about the mechanics of religious life; perhaps there are theology or language courses to be arranged; a lifetime of possessions has to be sorted, stored, given away, sold.

And the lucky young person about to embark on this new "career"? Sometimes they hardly seem any different from their brothers and sisters in college, no more pious, serious or noble; and, if anything, this is reassuring. One young man hoping to enter the Franciscans wonders about being able to keep up his fitness routine. He is relieved when he meets a young priest who belongs to a health club. Family members have many concerns. What about the telephone – will we be able to call her anytime? What will we do with his new car? Should we keep this furniture in case it doesn't work out? Can we visit the novitiate?* What do they wear?

And little by little, as we hear more stories of other young people, a human face appears on the community of religious. There's the gifted poet who has entered a contemplative order; the native person with two university degrees considering the priesthood; the young man who wants to be a lay brother, helping to care for the aged in his order.

---

* Young men or women wishing to enter a religious community often join a formation program while still living in their own homes. Afterwards, they may then spend a year in a convent, monastery or friary as a postulant (an official beginner) before entering a novitiate. The novices usually live somewhat more apart from the world to have time and tranquillity for prayer and study. After a very formal year or two in the novitiate (a home for novices) they will take temporary vows of poverty, chastity and obedience, and then usually return to studies of theology before taking final vows. Those wishing to be diocesan (or secular) priests live in a seminary and do not have a novitiate year. Nor do they take the simple (or temporary) vows.

Eventually, all of our very simple human preoccupations fall into place, and the great unknown starts to be less troubling to those who will be left behind. After all the hundreds of details are looked after – someone has to redirect the mail; another helps crate up the books going into storage – we are left with a great and glorious peace. Our family has been truly blessed by this special calling, a blessing we would wish to share with others, for we have not lost a son or daughter, a brother or sister, but have gained a whole worldwide network* of new friends working together, doing their human best to love and serve the Lord.

* Those who are considering the religious life have many options open to them these days, including teaching, counselling, missionary work, nursing and so on. There are different types of religious orders and institutes designed to meet these many and varied needs of the community.

Feast of the Ascension

The very last words of Matthew's gospel should be endlessly consoling to us so many years later: "Know that I am with you always; yes, to the end of time." Unfortunately, even today on the feast commemorating Christ's departure from the world, there is an unbidden question that sometimes comes to taunt and tease us in dark moments. Why didn't Jesus stay on earth long enough to establish a church; long enough to answer the questions that have bothered theologians for centuries; long enough to tell us how to keep going once he was not around any more?

Because of all those unanswered questions, there have been many fearful struggles between people of good will but opposing views since Jesus Christ departed this world in glory. The first disciples worried about the new gentile converts who had never been circumcised. The fourth and fifth centuries were marked by extensive controversies on the true nature of Christ, some claiming he was God but not man, others asserting he was human but not divine. The infamous thirteenth-century Inquisition* was like-

* In Mediaeval and Renaissance times, the imaginary line between sacred and secular powers was extremely hard to define. For this reason, people who held unorthodox religious views were considered to be not just out of step with the spiritual world but also a threat to the peace and stability of the civil order. Theoretically, this was the justification used for executing or imprisoning heretics. We no longer agree with this reasoning.

wise directed against "heretics" such as the Albigensians who held an assortment of unorthodox views. During the Reformation, the opposing sides argued long and violently about the pope, the sacraments, the laity, the bible, and just about every other issue that could be discussed.

Indeed, any outline of church history, dating right back to apostolic times, contains little more than the ongoing attempt to deal with the questions that have no obvious, indisputable answer. It seems that part of our salvation history is destined to be the struggle to formulate a detailed and wide-ranging understanding of those simple words, "a new commandment I give to you: to love one another."

Sometimes it is easy to turn away in disgust from the controversies that have raged in unseemly, even unChristian furore over so much of our history. And yet, we humans in our endless curiosity like to know. In the gospels, we can even see the apostles pestering Jesus, trying to pin him down for more details on the future of all things: "Lord, has the time come?" Their question went unheeded, but Christ gave them an answer all the same when he told them, "You will be my witnesses."

Inevitably, we will need to spend much energy coming to some understanding of this mission. Although the Fourth Gospel includes no description of the Ascension, it does record many of Jesus' farewell discourses. One that seems most fitting today, given so many centuries of controversy, bloodshed and intolerance, is in John 14:2: "There are many rooms in my father's house . . ."

Pentecost*

The Holy Spirit, like a shy heron lurking in the high reeds of some isolated marsh, seems to many of us an elusive being shrouded in mystery. And like the frustrated naturalist slogging through the early morning mist and tantalized by the far-off unearthly cry of some rare bird, we often hear a rumour of the Spirit's activities without ever getting a very clear picture of this most neglected member of the Trinity.

The world without the Spirit, we are told, would be marked by desolation and devastation, and many pessimistic critics of society (this or any other) are quick to point out that there is certainly an abundance of desolation and devastation on every hand. To those who dwell on the negative side of life here in the real world, there is little evidence of the work of the Holy Spirit in renewing, encouraging or inspiring a people seemingly unredeemable.

Yet for the first disciples, whose previous lives were marked by fear, distrust and a notable absence of any

* The "Feast of Weeks" in Old Testament times eventually came to be called "Pentecost" from the Greek word for fifty. It was celebrated at the time of the wheat harvest seven weeks (fifty days) after Passover. In Jewish tradition the Law was given to Moses on this day. Pentecost is also called "Whitsunday"; the origins of this ancient name are uncertain.

special heroism, the event of Pentecost had a very pronounced and immediate effect. Gathered together in their upper room, perhaps still timid after the departure of Jesus from their midst, the earth-shattering events of Good Friday and Easter still fresh in their memories, they were soon overwhelmed by the sound of a fierce wind which filled the house. Luke describes the visible appearance of the Spirit as "tongues of fire," an image that conveys something of the mystery and the power we associate with Pentecost.

And then, the amazing, astonishing change that comes over them – the torrents of eloquence, the prophetic speeches, the sign that something very real has happened to these ordinary men and women. Peter, who had betrayed his Lord three times just a little while before, has suddenly found a new and powerful voice within and begins to preach with determination, confidence and unfeigned zeal. Almost as an explanation for his own newfound abilities, his call to the multitudes for repentance includes the promise that the Holy Spirit would also come for them in baptism.

We, too, have been baptized and later confirmed, in ceremonies that were intended to herald the arrival of this sacred advocate into our hearts, yet our lives are often remarkable for their lack of virtue and understanding. Collectively and individually, we have stumbled and fallen on our journey, over and over again.

And yet we also pick ourselves up, over and over again. Cynics are quick to recognize sin and evil at work in the world; at the same time, there is ample proof that life is also a never-ending series of events marked by compassion, forgiveness, charity, understanding and fortitude. Perhaps these outward "good deeds" are but a token of some mysterious inner reality, evidence that we can somehow and sometimes hear more clearly the voice of the Spirit beckoning us to a new way. We are stirred, as it were, by a rush of heavenly wind, and warmed by the intense heat and light of a truth that really can burn, when we let it, with infinite power in our darkness.

Trinity Sunday

Over the centuries, devout peoples have incorporated a variety of unique gestures, special vestments and sacred vessels into their regular religious observances. These outward signs of our inward convictions have also allowed believers to identify more strongly with other members of the group, thus reinforcing the unity of the community, something especially helpful in difficult and troubled times. Many cultures, primitive and advanced, have expressed an astonishing variety of emotions through sacred dance. All over the world, there are religious festivals marked by the display of sacred objects and icons, the use of traditional clothing, the sounds of liturgical music.

The Church also has its share of outward traditions of age-old origin and purpose, but none is more widespread than the "sign of the cross." Included frequently in the mass, used to mark the beginning and the end of public and private prayer, a commemoration of one of the central truths of our faith, the sign of the cross is intimately familiar to every one of us, as familiar almost as our own names. How many thousands of times have we repeated this formula: "In the name of the Father and of the Son and of the Holy Spirit"? At the very end of Matthew's gospel, we hear these words as the risen Christ directs his apostles to go out to all nations, baptizing, teaching and observing the Lord's commandments.

While we are intimately familiar with this ritualized acknowledgement of the "three persons in one God," we are often at a loss for words to explain the Trinity except in the baldest, most simplistic terms. Some of us can go no further than the traditional teaching method of St. Patrick, who evidently used the three leaves of a shamrock to present the Trinity to the pagan Irish chieftains. Others can learnedly discuss the famous controversies accompanying the development of this doctrine, and the various councils[*] which attempted to describe and define this theological complexity. Neither approach is entirely satisfactory.

In recent times, using inclusive and non-sexist language, another formula for the sign of the cross has been proposed: "God the source of all being, the Eternal Word and the Holy Spirit" and our surprise on hearing this unexpected phrase may indeed jolt us into giving some thought to a prayer that is often just a mumbled and unconscious string of words. We are forced to focus on God as creator of all that is, ourselves included; God as Logos, word made flesh, come to earth as our redeemer and source of our new life; and God as Spirit, the fountain of the wisdom, grace and holiness that flows into us and transforms us.

---

[*] The Nicene Creed was written rather specifically to refute the position of the Arian heresy which claimed that Jesus Christ was not divine. It is not easy for *anyone* to understand the concept of three persons – the Father, the Son and the Holy Spirit – in one God, and various attempts to explain this problem have involved their authors in what we call heresy, or dogmatic unorthodoxy.

In the end, however, no amount of scholarly erudition or updated language can "explain" the Trinity to us, let alone prove its existence to the sceptical non-believer. Of all the components of Christianity, this is the one we are least able to grasp, the one best described as a mystery. The most we can hope for, it seems, is to leave ourselves open to the saving power and grace of this triune God, in order to experience that threefold force of creation, redemption and inspiration within ourselves, perhaps the best "proof" and explanation of all.

St. Joan of Arc

1412-1431

May 30

What has come to be called "The Hundred Years' War" was waged in fits and starts from 1337 to 1453. In its extremes of heroism and villainy – not to mention its conflicting aims and inconclusive results – this war is typical of most large-scale multinational struggles. Whatever the initial cause of the war – either the English claim to the French throne or the French rejection of the English claim, take your pick – eventually the fighting developed a momentum of its own. Fuelled by the prospect of rich plunder from their cavalry marches across France, the English were naturally reluctant to seek a diplomatic solution. The French, meanwhile, plagued by a lack of leadership, ended up as easy prey to the English incursions. And as in all mediaeval political situations, the web of arranged marriages, diplomatic alliances and feudal loyalties was further complicated by traditional rivalries, shifting allegiances and wicked treachery. All this confusion makes it very difficult for an outside observer to see where one side begins and the other ends. There are no clear-cut "good guys" or "bad guys."

Joan of Arc knew exactly where she stood when she arrived on the scene in her early teens, well into the eighth decade of the war. To her, the first step in solving the problem was to arrange a traditional coronation for the Dauphin in Rheims. She claimed that this was the message given to her in a vision by Saints Michael, Catherine and Margaret, and somehow, by a combination of sheer determination and military leadership, she succeeded. For a few short years, in company with the newly crowned king, she engaged in a number of victorious battles against the English, taking the first steps in successfully driving them out of France and rebuilding the country. Her presence in the campaign was in fact the turning point of a war which eventually was to peter out. France was more or less back in the hands of the French.

All good things come to an end, however, and one fine day Joan was captured by the Burgundians, sold to the English for 10,000 francs, tried for heresy and burned at the stake in Rouen, all before she was twenty years old. Today we are appalled by the accounts of her trial by the religious and civil authorities. As a matter of fact, many people back then were equally disgusted by the proceedings and, within thirty years of Joan's death, the verdict was overturned and she was vindicated.

Today, all Europe is moving away from the old concept of narrowly defined nation states and heading towards the newer vision of one community acknowledging many common interests and goals. Likewise, conventional warfare has been largely overshadowed by the worldwide threat of nuclear annihilation. In this climate, we are more impressed by peacemakers than military conquerors. During her short life, Joan of Arc was also searching for peace and, like many on that quest, she was a threat to the established wisdom of her day. As she understood things, "peace" had to include a duly anointed rightful king, French sovereignty in France and the withdrawal of English troops from French soil. Only a single-minded visionary, a nagging voice that could never be stilled, would have attempted that seemingly impossible program. This peasant girl, prophet and soldier is now revered as the patron saint of France.*

* Joan's story has been treated in various ways. Because he was on the English side, Shakespeare describes her as a witch; Schiller sees her as a romantic heroine; George Bernard Shaw makes her into a good Protestant nationalist. On the silver screen, actresses as varied as Maria Falconetti, Jean Seberg and Ingrid Bergman have taken this role.

Corpus Christi

(The Solemnity of the Body and Blood of Christ)

Parishes have traditionally organized their First Communion celebrations in the spring and, like everything else in the world, customs change, fashions come and go, our points of view shift. The older generations can look back with pride and fondness to a Sunday morning thirty, forty, fifty years ago, and remember that new blue suit or white dress and veil, a first pair of grown-up shoes, gifts of rosaries, little missals and holy cards. The fear of fainting may have loomed large in those of us uneasy in our hot stuffy churches and now uncomfortably hungry after fasting from midnight. Very few of us, however, recall an explosion of religious ecstasy that we somehow expected would attend this emotionally charged experience when we would receive "Baby Jesus" for the first time.*

The years pass by and we are indisputably older and greyer, thinner or fatter depending on how our genes take us. Some of us are still going to church. And if we look around us at communion time, we may even find that we have learned something over our lifetime, something that no one ever suggested back in Grade One.

---

* We believe that Jesus Christ is really present in the bread and wine consecrated at mass, not just symbolically present. This mystery was a source of great concern to many troubled and sincere people during the Reformation, some of whom on both sides of the issue were prepared to die for their beliefs.

A large and busy parish at ten o'clock on a Sunday morning may not seem the best place in the world in which to await an earth-moving religious experience. Invariably, the building is too hot or too cold. There is bound to be at least one crying baby or fidgety toddler nearby. In the next pew, someone is mumbling the responses and singing off-key.

On the other hand, when we look around prepared to find good in what we see, we may notice that the same crying baby is being held and comforted by a mother or father who has made a special point to get to that mass, maybe even with another youngster in tow. The poor soul with the unsteady voice may be slightly out of step with those praying and singing nearby; surely we have the charity to accept that in congregational worship sincere effort is the only thing that counts. The building itself, whether graceful or ugly, a tribute to architectural harmony or a travesty of discordant space, has become home to a disparate group of individuals who may be strangers to one another on the street, but in church are linked together by a common purpose, however imperfectly understood or haltingly articulated.

As we gather to praise and glorify our God, we may remember that the experience we are sharing has been marked out by a sacrifice begun in the covenant with Moses; a priesthood with origins in New Testament times; prayers that are centuries old; a tradition that has inspired and sustained ordinary men and women, as well as poets, saints and scholars, for nearly two thousand years. We may also remember that our common understanding of this event we call the mass has developed and evolved from apostolic times; there have been unhappy periods when the value and nature of congregational participation was under dispute; there has been bitterness instead of harmony.

But as we see at our First Communion Sundays, times do change. The chaste white dresses and simple navy blazers of our childhood memories have been replaced by a rainbow of colour, funky stockings, outlandish jewellery and unthinkable hairstyles. The ordinary men and women in the pews now speak up boldly, giving voice to responses that all of us understand and most of us even know by heart. There are lay people reading from the scriptures, leading the singing, distributing communion. And what gladdens the hearts of sensitive churchgoers as we stand before the altar is that we are all still there, rooted in the past, living in the present and looking towards the future. Together.

The Visitation

May 31

The Bible, among its many treasures, contains a great number of stories about journeys, some dating right back to the days of the patriarchs 2000 years before the birth of Christ. The semi-nomadic tribes that were to become the chosen people of God crisscrossed the lands of the Near East, notably in the area between present-day Israel and Egypt. Some of their trips were part of the great movements of population brought on by famine or economic pressure. Later on, the exodus led by Moses to the Promised Land was inspired by a desire to escape the oppression of unsympathetic overlords in Egypt. In New Testament times, Paul sailed around the Mediterranean to visit the new churches established in Antioch, Ephesus, Corinth and Rome. Common to all these excursions, pilgrimages and expeditions was the conviction that they were inspired by lofty ideals and marked by serious high purpose.

Today's feast likewise commemorates a voyage of great importance: Mary's visit to her cousin Elizabeth. This trip, called the "Visitation," was in confirmation of the prophecy of the Angel Gabriel at the time of the Annunciation, for Mary has been told that her cousin, in spite of an unlikely old age, has conceived a son. Knowing that all things are possible to the Lord, Mary immediately sets off on her visit. Luke's gospel certainly describes the reunion between the two women in terms suitably appropriate for the Mother of the Saviour conversing with the Mother of a Prophet. The stately and beautiful language of the Magnificat,* Mary's canticle of praise and thanksgiving, is based on a prayer by Hannah, another special biblical mother, and was composed in happy anticipation of the most holy of births.

Undoubtedly, Luke's purpose in his stylized description of Mary is to remind his readers of the unique and special nature of her baby who will be called "son of the Most High." Similarly, the presentation of Elizabeth is highlighted by the unusual circumstances also surrounding her pregnancy, for her son, to be known as John the Baptist, was sent to make ready the way of the Lord.

Underneath the biblical language, the echoes from a variety of Old Testament sources and the prophetic nature of nearly every sentence, there is a real human story. A young woman leaves her home in Galilee in the north of Palestine and heads south into the hill country of Judah, a journey of perhaps a hundred miles or more. We don't know how she travelled, on foot perhaps or as part of a caravan, probably not alone, more likely with unnamed relatives. Journeys, then and now, always involve anxiety, excitement, preparation and adventure, especially in those faraway days of highway bandits, rough roads and uncomfortable inns. Of course Elizabeth gives

---

* The Magnificat has been part of the Vespers (evening prayer) service since the sixth century. Bach, Monteverdi and others have composed wonderful musical settings for this canticle (or song-like prayer).

her kinswoman an ecstatic welcome when she finally arrives; as Luke puts it so quaintly, the babe leapt in her womb. Living in the time before regular mail delivery, telephones or fax machines, Elizabeth may have had no previous warning about the visit!

You can also be assured that Mary and Elizabeth found time to share their common concerns at the very real dangers of childbirth, Mary as a young first-time mother, Elizabeth, older and at greater risk. They stayed together for three months and Mary left when her own pregnancy would have been more evident, to repeat the journey on the dusty roads back to Nazareth. She would have been sustained and refreshed, not only by the sentiments expressed in all those beautiful prayers, but also by the very real human companionship and comfort that we, too, celebrate on this day.

Sacred Heart

(First Friday after Corpus Christi)

Sometimes in the early spring, travellers in the rugged mountain areas of central Italy will come upon a nomadic shepherd wandering purposefully with his flock from winter quarters to summer pastures, using the ancient tracks that still exist in some of the more remote corners of the countryside. These Abruzzese shepherds, like their sheep, are a hardy bunch, living close to the land with only a couple of intelligent dogs for company, camping out in all weather, prepared for every emergency, really a relic of a bygone era in these days of agribusiness and large-scale farming.

When Jesus told his parable of the good shepherd, his audience would have been instantly familiar with the cares and preoccupations of one tending a flock. After all, the world of the Old Testament is full of nomadic pastoralists – Abraham, Isaac, Jacob – measuring their wealth in flocks of sheep and goats; carefully watering their animals at wells in the arid countryside; moving to new ground in times of famine; giving the first fruits of their labour as sacrifices and burnt offerings on the altar of the Lord.

And to a people intimately familiar with this life, the picture drawn of the good shepherd would be immediate and powerful. The New Testament audience could readily imagine a man used to life outdoors, strong enough to defend the flock against roaming predators (human and animal), yet capable of tending the newborn lambs with gentleness, ready for just about anything.

This image of Christ as our shepherd is presented to us in some of the readings associated with the Sacred Heart,* a day commemorating the loving concern that each of us receives as part of Jesus' flock. The good shepherd theme is reinforced by other familiar writings such as Psalm 23, which says, "The Lord is my Shepherd," the Old Testament expression of a God who is personally concerned with our welfare.

If Jesus' audience could easily understand his portrait of the shepherd, our own troubled times should have no difficulty relating to the plight of the lost sheep. As the parable states, the shepherd will leave the ninety-nine that are safe to search the wilderness for the one that is lost "until he finds it." Day after day, individually and collectively, we experience a wilderness of disappointment, injustice, violence and human misery, attacked on all sides by predators as varied as ill-health, economic chaos and political instability. No wonder we sometimes feel lost! The feast of the Sacred Heart is meant to remind us that, all the while, whether we know it or not, someone – someone with infinite patience and concern – is out there looking for us.

---

* This way of describing Jesus' loving concern is a relatively new observance, dating from the seventeenth century when St. Margaret Mary Alacoque through her mystical experiences drew attention to this love using the image of the Sacred Heart.

St. Anthony of Padua

1195-1231

June 13

The great thirteenth-century figure of St. Anthony of Padua has been venerated in the hearts of millions of people for over 750 years. Societies worldwide honour his name and establish charities* in direct imitation of his life and work; processions and special parish celebrations still take place in June to honour his feast day. Padua remains a popular place of pilgrimage, where a magnificent basilica serves as a tomb and memorial to the man called the "Ark of the Testament," the "Hammer of the Heretics" and the "Evangelical Doctor."

Rarely do we remember that this immensely popular saint started life in another country with another name and, instead of the familiar habit of St. Francis, wore the black and white of an Augustinian canon** for ten years. Switching careers in midstream is not just a twentieth-century phenomenon.

In any case, our story of "Anthony" starts in Portugal where he was born the eldest son of a noble family, and

* The mediaeval custom of giving St. Anthony's bread to the poor has been updated today to include help for the unemployed, the sick and the needy, especially in developing countries.

** "Canon" comes from a Greek word for rule, norm, standard, measure. In this instance, it refers to a member of a religious order established by a "rule."

while still Fernando Martino entered an Augustinian house near Lisbon, eventually transferring to Coimbra in order to have more peace and solitude for prayer and study. Great things were evidently expected from him because of his marked intellectual abilities and phenomenal memory.

But like many of us who start off in the wrong place at the right time, Fernando felt something was missing. The arrival of some Franciscan friars to the door of his monastery begging for alms seems to have been the answer to an unspoken prayer, and he jumped at the chance to join up with them. These were the very early days of organized religious life, and he was welcomed with open arms, without even the formality of time in a novitiate. And thus he became "Anthony" in honour of the place where his new life began: a poor monastery dedicated to St. Anthony of Egypt.

His goal at this stage was to go out as a missionary to the Moslem communities in North Africa, perhaps even to become a martyr for the faith. Instead, he arrived in Morocco, instantly fell seriously ill and, in shame and embarrassment, was forced to head back home to Portugal without preaching a single word. Before he got back, his ship was caught in a severe storm and blown wildly off course, to land eventually in Sicily hundreds of miles from his original destination.

From these inauspicious beginnings, there developed a remarkable life: as a preacher he could hold the attention of vast outdoor crowds in the days before microphones and audio-visual aids; as a teacher his early studies served him well and he is considered the first Franciscan theologian; as a holy man of God, pages and pages of miracles are ascribed to him, including the wonderful story of the fishes in the river gathering to hear him speak. Simple country people as well as learned scholars and the nobility were moved by his words and his works. Yet he spent only ten years as a Franciscan friar, some of them in obscurity in a mountain hermitage; some in France combatting the Albigensians, with his voice his only weapon; altogether a very short time in which to establish such a prodigious reputation.

Padua as his last home now claims our attention as the site of his shrine, and rightly so because he loved it. He would be equally revered in any place dedicated to those whose way is marked by false starts, sudden detours, surprising interruptions and unexpected destinations.

Birthday of John the Baptist

June 24

When we speak of a saint's "feast day" we usually mean the day established by history or tradition to celebrate the end of an earthly life and the beginning of a heavenly one. Besides Jesus on Christmas Day, two special people are also honoured on their birthdays, Mary on September 8 and John the Baptist today.* Universal reverence for the Baptist has been part of church tradition since very early times, dating back to the fourth century. The story of this John, the long-hoped-for son born to Elizabeth and Zechariah, is told at great length at the very beginning of Luke's gospel, and all the other evangelists include some of his adventures in their narratives. His death is mentioned by Josephus, a contemporary historian of the Jewish people, and indeed his martyrdom is a familiar subject in art and even opera!

In Renaissance paintings, John the Baptist usually looks like the first hippie, dressed in animal skins, long haired, half-naked and wild-eyed, not surprising for one who had camped out in the wilderness living on locusts and wild honey for some time. His call to repentance, borrowed from Isaiah, "Make straight the way of the Lord," was evidently presented in a strongly persuasive manner for disciples flocked to him. Even Herod, his enemy,

* St-Jean-Baptiste Day is still celebrated in Quebec as a civic holiday.

found it interesting to talk to him, and appears to have ordered his execution with some reluctance.

Much of John's preaching, as reported by the gospels, has a decidedly apocalyptic flavour, inspired no doubt by his heightened consciousness of the retribution at hand for our unworthiness. Human nature being what it is, there seems to be a need for every generation to produce a "voice crying in the wilderness" leading the people back onto the path of righteousness.

At the same time, John recognized himself as but a humble servant of a higher master. "I am not fit to untie the strap of his sandals" is his poetic way of referring to his cousin, the one whom we know as the Christ. And yet Jesus submits himself to be baptized by John in the River Jordan. Surely the Son of God did not need to be cleansed of non-existent sins in any purifying waters; and, as Matthew describes it, John himself remarks at this reversal of their roles: "It is I who need baptism from you." Perhaps now we are in a better position to understand Jesus' actions on that day at the very beginning of his ministry. Fear, pain, hunger, desire – we easily accept that Jesus should have participated with us in the full range of human emotions. In his baptism, we also see our Saviour joining with us – all sinful humanity – in this public act of repentance and reconciliation, this collective acknowledgment of his Father.

And so Jesus is baptized by his cousin. The words of the Almighty thunder from the clouds, the Holy Spirit descends and we now recognize in this scene a graphic presentation of the Trinity. On this day, the birthday of John the Baptist, we may also find ourselves remembering the fact of our own baptisms, no doubt less dramatic than the events which took place on the bank of the River Jordan. Nevertheless, we too struggle and strain throughout our lives to hear the approval in a heavenly voice that will say to us, "Here are all my children. I am pleased."

Saints Peter and Paul

June 29

In the third century in Rome, in a society so very different from our own that few of us can even imagine an ordinary day there, the Church began celebrating the feast of Saints Peter and Paul, to commemorate their martyrdom* during Nero's infamous persecutions around 64 A.D. We have grown accustomed ever since to thinking of these two as a pair, having seen them grouped together in countless religious paintings, Peter holding his two keys, the symbol of authority, Paul with the book representing his writings.

Nevertheless, the two men couldn't be more different in background: Peter, the uneducated Galilean fisherman, often mentioned first in the gospel narratives, headstrong and impulsive, yet obviously a leader; Paul, the Roman citizen, highly educated, familiar with the Greek language, philosophy and culture, fully capable of theological subtlety, a born teacher. Peter, the eyewitness to the events of Jesus' public ministry and his triumph over death, intimately linked with the Jerusalem community; Paul, the former enemy of the new religion, only a believer after a personal conversion experience, now called by the title "Apostle to the Gentiles."

---

* Peter is believed to have suffered martyrdom through crucifixion. Paul as a Roman citizen was allowed to be beheaded instead.

While we relish the contrast between these two gigantic figures, there is something inescapably fitting about the bond between them that this day highlights. Paul's letters, as part of the bible, are recognized as inspired, and are revered through our faith as unique and special writings. Peter is now described as the first pope, in recognition of the founding of the Church as an institution. God has revealed himself to us in many ways, including through the lives and works of these saints. They are part of our Christian belief, a belief that centres on Jesus – Peter's friend, Paul's former enemy – the ultimate manifestation of God in the world.

Neither Peter nor Paul would have been able to imagine us sitting around today, thinking and writing about them, as they were convinced that Jesus' second coming was close at hand. However, the end of the world did not materialize as expected, the Good News continued its spread and today millions of people around the world call themselves Christians.* From small communities in age-old Mediterranean seaports and towns, to lands whose very existence was unknown to the ancient world, the message has travelled and endured, through persecutions, controversies, scandals and upheavals, not to mention waves of indifference, for all these centuries.

A large downtown parish in a North American city might seem to be light years away from a small gathering of the faithful in a private home in New Testament Rome or Corinth. Yet we are still singing hymns of praise,

* We were first described as Christians in 43 A.D. in Antioch, capital of Syria. The term was considered an insult.

reading the word of God, and breaking bread together. If our faith has endured, it may be due to some of the things that we have inherited through Peter and Paul: the principle of continuity and leadership, built upon a Rock, acting in harmony with the True Word revealed to humanity, all for the benefit of the pilgrim Church on earth.

St. Benedict

c. 480-547

July 11

Just about everything associated with St. Benedict is so interesting or edifying that it is hard to know where to start. With his Rule, masterpiece of common sense and organizational genius, the foundation of Western monasticism? With the network of Benedictine monasteries that spread across Europe in his wake, contributing an immense amount to the preservation and dissemination of culture after the fall of Rome? With the pious stories that are associated with him – the three tame ravens, the miracles of healing, the attempted (and foiled) poisonings? Perhaps it is easiest to see something of the Benedict common to all three traditions in Subiaco, the place in central Italy where he started off and itself a source of great pleasure to the visitor today.

When Benedict, like so many other well-off young people then and now, turned away from the degenerate world and retired in disgust and austerity, he ended up in Subiaco, an old Roman site blessed with remote caves and towering evergreen forests. And in spite of his initial plan to embrace solitude, he soon found himself preaching to the shepherds, then ministering to a small flock of like-minded disciples and eventually founding twelve monasteries in the neighbouring area. Thus and so his fame spread, and in time, led by the aforementioned ravens, he travelled southwest to Monte Cassino, where he founded the monastery that was to become the flagship house of the "Benedictines."

Monte Cassino was bombed to smithereens in the Second World War, and its subsequent reconstruction, though admirable, is not inspiring. In Subiaco, however, there remains the series of chapels clawed out of the rocky mountain fastness in the early Middle Ages by those not only loyal to Benedict's memory, but inspired to commemorate it in a series of spectacular frescoes on the walls of the chapels and grottoes. In the Cave of the Shepherds, one can still see a fragment of a seventh-century painting of Our Lady. Other wonderful works include a portrait of a famous visitor to the monastery: Francis of Assisi, dating from the days when he was still "Brother Francis," not yet the patron saint of Italy.

Artistic representations of Benedict's life often include the three tame ravens, symbols of the divine inspiration that led him from the remote and limited opportunities in the mountains to the wide world he would encounter in Monte Cassino. We also know that he left the site of his first foundations after he was hounded and harassed by a jealous local priest. His virtues made other enemies as well; the dissolute monks of one abbey which he attempted to reform tried to rid themselves of his righteous interference by poison. They failed, either through heavenly intervention or their own ineptitude, and Benedict lived on to write his famous Rule. This extremely successful handbook for the organization of a monastic community is full of common sense wisdom and sets forth in detail a plan for the intelligent guidance of a lifetime of days devoted to prayer, manual labour and study.

After visiting this wonderful abbey, one can easily recognize the tradition of learning, worship, culture and service long associated with the name of Benedict. His spirit is still present, not just in these magnificent paintings and entertaining legends, but in the many visitors who take the time to search out and pray in this spot made special, not through superstition, but from an ongoing reverence for all that is holy and beautiful.*

---

* St. Benedict is further honoured in that much of what we know of his life was written by another special monk, Pope St. Gregory the Great.

The Transfiguration

August 6

"It is well that we are here." These are Peter's words on Mount Tabor as he and his companions awake to see their Master, his face changed, his clothing a dazzling white, talking to Moses and Elijah. We have difficulty explaining the mystical experience that took place in the event we now call the Transfiguration. In the Old Testament, the Lord's presence was frequently demonstrated to the Israelites in the form of a cloud; likewise in this episode in Jesus' life, we find a cloud descending onto the mountaintop. In Exodus we read about Moses, his face shining, as he came down from Mount Sinai carrying the Ten Commandments in stone, after talking directly with Yahweh. Similarly Jesus' face and clothing are charged with a supernatural light after his experience.

All three synoptic gospels* provide the briefest description for this altered state that so closely echoes the direct experience that Moses had of God, but they still leave many of our concerns unanswered. What kind of prayers was Jesus saying when it happened? Did he know about this beforehand? Did he do this all the time? What

---

* The gospels of Matthew, Mark and Luke are called synoptic, meaning "with the same eye" because they tell many of the same stories and agree on many of the details of the life of Jesus.

did he really learn from his conversation with the two long-dead prophets?

The gospel writers showed little apparent interest in the aspects of this event that trouble those who habitually look for rational explanations of unusual phenomena. Instead, they let Peter, ever the one with a ready answer, step onto centre stage and speak his beautiful line: "It is well that we are here."

Perhaps Peter doesn't understand what is happening around him. Maybe his only suggestions in this crisis are foolish ones. Even if he can't describe what he did; even if no one ever finds out what he saw for a long time to come; somehow, it is important that he participated, perhaps as a witness so that his own faith will be strengthened; perhaps as a witness so that future generations may also believe.

Peter, the rock upon which the Church is built, so often speaks with a voice just like ours: sometimes frail and unsteady, sometimes courageous and bold. And in a situation plainly outside his normal experience of life, he finds a few simple words to express a faith and hope challenged by events that fill him with awe and fear and that he cannot readily understand. "It is well that we are here."

The Assumption of the Blessed Virgin Mary

August 15

In the Vatican Museum, there is a large painting by the young Raphael of the Coronation of the Virgin, once part of a large altarpiece commissioned for the church of San Francesco in Perugia. The central portion of the altarpiece is divided in two: in the top half, surrounded by cherubs and angels playing musical instruments, the Virgin sits beside her son who places a crown on her head. In the bottom half, "on earth," lies a large empty tomb around which the disciples are gathered, some staring down into the empty stone coffin, some looking heavenward. There is St. Peter with his keys, St. John looking very young and clasping his gospel, St. Paul holding a sword and a book. Out of the empty tomb, as if from an oversized window box, grows a profusion of large upright flowers including a lily blessed with a cluster of blossoms. All in all, a composition of charm and grace and, along with its companion panels, it forms a very impressive memorial to several events in Mary's life.

Many centuries later, the altarpiece no longer adorns a church but is preserved in a museum. The realistically painted flowers growing in the empty tomb withered ages ago, if they ever existed at all. And wherever and however Mary is these days, she doesn't seem to be here on earth.

The virtues that she embodied – gentle maternal love, patience in suffering, courageous acceptance of God's will – are not strongly revered by many members of the human race.*

Ironically, we continue to enjoy an artistic legacy formed in past centuries by those devoted to her name and image. Besides the aforementioned Raphael, the world's museums are stuffed full of paintings of her life by every major and minor name in art history. The numbers of tourists per year to the cathedrals built in her honour, with Notre-Dame de Paris, Chartres and Rouen leading the way, are staggering to contemplate. And our musical language has been enriched by countless works composed in her honour, from the Marian motets of the early Middle Ages to the setting of "Ave Maria" by Schubert.

These many and varied artistic flowers have never faded, regardless of our contemporary neglect of the person of Mary. And it is Mary as a person – that mysterious fusion of body and soul – who is remembered today. If it is fitting that Mary, her body as well as her soul, should be enthroned in a heavenly setting, as we believe, it is equally fitting that we should recognize the dignity of ourselves, body as well as soul.

The world around us may be willing to ignore the bodily claims of vast numbers of human beings, the need for food, shelter and clean water. There may be fanatics

---

* Although the dogma of the Assumption (declaring that Mary was received body and soul into heaven after her death) was only proclaimed officially in 1950, there has long been a feast commemorating this very special privilege granted to her as the Mother of God.

who want us to focus exclusively on only one limited aspect of our nature. We ourselves may forget that every side of our being deserves some of our attention. As Mary's Son himself reminded us, we were made to love the Lord our God with our heart, our soul, our mind and our strength, in other words, with every gift, virtue, treasure and quality that combine to form us as uniquely human, "body and soul."

St. Monica

c. 323-387

August 27

Just outside Rome, on the road to Leonardo Da Vinci Airport, are the vast excavations of Ostia Antica. Lucky visitors wander peacefully among the wildflowers, investigating the ruins and musing about life under the emperors, untroubled by the crowds who fight to see many of the same things in more popular sites such as Pompeii and Herculaneum. As in all these ancient cities, the remains of baths, theatres, shops and houses are still visible; there is even a well-preserved café, complete with marble shelves and elegant decorations, an establishment that would not look out of place on the Via Veneto today.

Ostia Antica was once a busy port. In another part of the ruins one can find a little plaque with a simple Latin inscription reminding us that St. Monica died here while she and her son, St. Augustine, were waiting to embark for North Africa after a long and tiring journey through Italy.

Monica's life seems to have been somewhat less tranquil than the quiet, brick-lined paths and grassy hillsides that remain behind in Ostia to beguile the visitor today. Married to a hot-tempered pagan philanderer, mother of a brilliant but wayward son, caught in a long-lasting debate over one of the dangerous popular heresies,* Monica seems to have had her share of troubles here on earth. At some point, however, her patience, her tears, her prayers and her good example were rewarded: the husband converted to Christianity, the son forsook his evil ways and Monica had cause to rejoice. Not long after Augustine's baptism, when she caught the fever that was to be her final illness, she said that all her hopes in the world had been fulfilled.

Some years later, when Augustine was a bishop and the tireless defender of the Church, he set himself down to record the story of his conversion in that rambling collection of prayers, reminiscences and philosophical musings called *The Confessions.* Here we learn many things about his mother, for Augustine takes plenty of time to tell us the story of Monica's life, complete with anecdotes about her wise old governess, suspicious mother-in-law, bad-tempered husband and quarrelsome friends.

The popular image of St. Augustine that has come down to us today is that of a stern moralist, suspicious of women and rather too inclined to dwell on the gloomy side of life. The stories he has written about his mother, however, are very different. Most touching of all is his description of the vision they shared together one evening in Ostia "while looking out a window." Their conversation seems to have led them to a "place" far beyond the

---

* Augustine, like many others of his time, had been a follower of the Manichean heresy. The Manichees believed that the ancient struggle between Light and Darkness was the source of the corresponding Good and Evil in today's world. Augustine was eventually converted through the inspirational preaching of St. Ambrose, bishop of Milan.

dwelling where they sat musing about philosophy and staring into the garden.

A few days after this profoundly moving and mystical experience, Monica passed away. Her love and concern for her troublesome son and difficult husband are entirely familiar themes to many of us today. So also are the pain and grief felt by the friends and relatives she left behind her. Equally familiar is Augustine's recognition of the conflict between the human anguish he feels at the loss of his mother, and his belief in a world he cannot see but knows only through faith.

It is fitting that August 27 should be dedicated to the memory of Monica, the woman who inspired such devotion; the very next day is marked on our calendars in honour of her son, Augustine.

St. Gregory the Great

(Pope Gregory I, c. 540-604)

September 3

The tomb of St. Gregory is in the west aisle of St. Peter's in Rome under one of the less distinguished altars, somewhat removed from the grander memorial creations ordered (or at least inspired) by later popes who had more concern for their dignity in death. A small carved marble casket contains whatever bones can remain after nearly 1400 years of quiet decay, and over the altar there is a large but uninteresting mosaic depicting one of the miracles attributed to the saint. The true memorial to Gregory's work and achievement lies elsewhere.

This well-born Roman (he was acclaimed pope by the popular demand of the local clergy and people) ascended the throne of St. Peter with some reluctance, evidently preferring a more retired life in the Benedictine monastery he had founded with his considerable inheritance. In testimony to his views on the papacy, he described himself as "the servant of the servants of God," the first pope to use this title and one later revived by John XXIII.

He seems to have been truly committed to the welfare of the Church, especially concerned with the education of the clergy and, to this end, he wrote extensively. Left behind is a vast collection of his letters, lives of the saints and scriptural commentaries. The effect of his writing was felt for centuries. Nearly 300 years after his death, King Alfred himself translated from Latin to Anglo-Saxon one of Gregory's letters on "pastoral care" and had it sent round to every diocese in England!

In addition to the theological excellence which has merited for him the title, "Doctor of the Church," Gregory left one further memorial behind, in the form of the vast body of chant which he began to collect and organize and is now called "Gregorian" in his honour. Legend has it that Gregory actually composed the chants while an angel whispered in his ear; contemporary musicologists suggest that he intended to establish a standard, orderly form for use in all churches. With the spread of Christianity, this core of Roman liturgical music, remarkable for its graceful beauty and haunting simplicity, was expanded. Furthermore, it formed the basis of many other works, both sacred and secular, throughout the Middle Ages and the Renaissance.

In the end, all of us whose lives have been touched by music are greatly in Gregory's debt for the order that he sought to bring to his vast liturgical inheritance. Our musical language has its roots in those far-off centuries when hooded monks and nuns chanted the Hours of the Divine Office in drafty Romanesque abbeys, using the modes and melodies that Gregory had collected. Those chants stand at the beginning of a tradition that would grow and develop in later times, to the delight of all of us who can today appreciate the poetic richness of a symphony, the subtle control of a chamber sonata and the soaring splendour of an oratorio.*

---

* Legend also tells us that Gregory once saw some fair-haired Anglo-Saxon slaves in the market and, concerned for their spiritual welfare, he made the memorable comment, "Not Angles but Angels." He then sent a fellow Benedictine, St. Augustine of Canterbury, to preach the gospel in England.

Triumph of the Cross

September 14

St. Helena, daughter of an innkeeper, wife of a Roman general, and mother of an emperor, has been credited by such a reliable source as St. Ambrose with finding the true cross around the year 326 A.D. Fragments of this most holy of relics have been revered ever since in churches around the world, including a few slivers displayed at St. Michael's Cathedral in Toronto. There is no doubt that the existence of a sacred object of the significance of the true cross would galvanize public imagination and provide an irresistible focus for devotion by the faithful. Even an age as jaded and indifferent as our own has shown keen interest in the possessions which the rich and/or famous have left behind. Our ongoing fascination with the contemporary artifacts previously owned by the likes of the Duchess of Windsor, Andy Warhol, Liberace and Elvis is proof of that.

Our thoughts today are inescapably led, however, from the actual wood of the true cross excavated somewhere on a Palestinian hillside, to the symbolic cross under whose banner Constantine, son of the intrepid Helena,* vanquished his opponents to become emperor. For Constantine, whose life and times would have been a

* Helena also founded important churches on the Mount of Olives and in Bethlehem, and was noted for her kindness to soldiers, the needy and the imprisoned.

fitting subject for the cameras of Cecil B. DeMille, was the first decidedly Christian ruler. Regardless of his motives, a mixture of the political and the religious, he was clearly the source of the acts of toleration ending the persecution of the Christians. He took it upon himself to construct new churches throughout the Empire; he was the one who called the first ecumenical council at Nicea, the council responsible for the formulation of an orthodox creed still recited today.* In other words, under Constantine's protection the great leap from "persecuted underground sect" to "official state-supported religion" takes place.

This immense alteration in their prospects drastically influenced the early Christians' outlook on life. Instead of an almost certain crown of martyrdom, the popes eventually found themselves wearing the triple tiara. Instead of intimate gatherings of worship in private homes or small obscure churches, the faithful were soon to experience the liturgy in wonderful public buildings decorated with precious mosaics and frescoes. Soon it became politically advantageous to be known as a member of the new religion. Christianity had become part of the establishment.

And likewise, it seems a whole new set of values became important in the changing "Christian ideal." At one time the earliest converts had to be physically brave in the face of martyrdom; intensely committed to the faith they might be called upon to witness with their lives; even somewhat adept in organizing their lives in clandestine

---

* The Nicene Creed (formally called the Creed of Nicea-Constantinople) is a more complex theological statement than the shorter Apostles' Creed also said at mass.

communities. Now, after Constantine, there is a distinct change. The Church will find it wants a more carefully defined theology to accommodate its growing numbers; a more highly developed structure which can respond to its new position in the world; a body of sacred art, literature and music to draw its members closer together, as the early "eyewitness" stories fade farther and farther into the past.

These inevitable shifts in emphasis, for good and ill, changed the early Church. There have been further adaptations throughout the centuries in response to the waxing and waning of the spiritual and temporal power of the popes. We survived the Reformation, the modern scientific revolution and two World Wars; we have lived through challenges, victories, defeats. A body of truth has remained in the hearts and lives of believers, the real tribute to the "triumph of the cross," far more important than any basilicas, chapels and shrines dedicated to the sacred relics remembered today.

The Archangels Michael, Gabriel and Raphael

September 29

What is an angel? In spite of our familiarity with these heavenly beings through art, literature and popular culture – witness the existence of Angel Food Cake, *Paradise Lost,* and paintings of the Annunciation – giving an intelligent answer that will satisfy every twentieth-century believer is very difficult.

What does an angel do? Now we are on surer ground, because an angel functions primarily as a messenger of the Almighty and the very word *angelos* means "messenger" in Greek. The bible is full of references to angels and their activities: rescuing Isaac from sacrifice; saving Daniel in the lion's den; ministering to Jesus after his temptation in the desert. In fact, there was an explosion of interest in angels in Jewish culture during the years immediately before Jesus' birth. The apocryphal Book of Enoch* contains much esoteric information about angels and their existence; this book is even quoted in the Epistle of Jude, and was well known at Qumram, home of the Dead Sea Scrolls.

---

* A number of these ancient writings superficially resemble the books of the bible. Some contain information that was once widely accepted as "true," including material on the childhood of Jesus, the nature of angels, and so on. These apocryphal books are of interest to scholars but for many reasons were rejected for inclusion in our bible.

September 29, originally devoted only to St. Michael and thus called "Michaelmas," today honours all three archangels mentioned in the bible. Michael is traditionally regarded as the leader of the heavenly army that battles Satan. We often see him in his Roman style armour, the conqueror of the dragon from Revelation, a symbol of strength and might, God's messenger of law and judgement. Gabriel, whose name means "God's hero," is associated with prophecy, wisdom, understanding and good news, a messenger of mercy and promise. It is Gabriel, with his beautiful wings and gorgeous flowing robes, who is seen in all those paintings kneeling to Mary and addressing her as the future mother of God. Finally, there is Raphael, the messenger of healing and reconciliation, the companion of Tobias in his adventures, the one who could cure blindness and drive away unclean spirits. His name, appropriately enough, means "God heals."

We can learn virtually nothing reliable about the nature of these magnificent beings from all the sources open to us, other than the splendid names given to their choirs: seraphim, cherubim, thrones, dominations, principalities, powers, virtues, archangels and angels. From the accounts given of their activities while caring for their charges, however, we can learn much. And, as always, everything we learn leads us back to an understanding of the Lord as a God of power and might, of infinite concern for his people, the source of all that is wonderful here on earth and in heaven above.

St. Francis of Assisi

1182-1226

October 4

Francis of Assisi preached to the birds. He called the sun his brother and the moon his sister. He embraced Lady Poverty as his mistress and died with the marks of the stigmata on his body.

We know these and a thousand other facts about him because he was recognized in his own lifetime as someone special. His followers were eager to compose his biography as a testimony to his sanctity. Indeed, when it appeared he was dying, there was even concern at what we would call the "civic level" that his still living body be safeguarded as a source of future relics. Some of the stories of Francis and his miracles are more plausible than others; nevertheless, peaking from behind the legends that have grown up around him there emerges the face of a recognizable human being.

Francis certainly preached to the birds. In fact, he seemed to be forever talking to everything in the world around him, not because he was a lovable eccentric or the first ecologist but because he knew that everything under the sun owed its existence to the Lord. Likewise, Francis found himself devoted to music and dance, not for reasons of aesthetics but because his whole life was an act of praise to God. And what better way to express one's joy in life and creation than through hymns, psalms and canticles? He died singing. His inability to put on a sombre face while waiting for the "guest to whom no man opens the door willingly" was a source of annoyance to those unable to understand the breadth of his spirit.*

On the other hand, Francis' life also contained its share of tears – tears inspired by meditation on his Lord's passion and suffering; tears of frustration and annoyance over the dissension that eventually developed among his followers; even tears at Christmas in remembrance of Mary giving birth in poverty and neglect. Ill health, sadness and doubt, the subversion of his blessed ideals of poverty and simplicity: these also were his companions, just as much as the falcons, the tame wolves and the larks that he befriended.

Over and over again, whether in joy or sorrow, Francis returned to his grand theme – a desire to venerate, indeed imitate, Christ in his own life. Poverty was so desirable because it was the state in which his Lord had lived. The crèche was inspiring because it re-created the scene of the blessed babe's birth.** The psalms were sung because they gave glory to God and because Jesus too had said them. His letters and writings overflow with quotations from the gospels as if the holy words were never very far from his thoughts.

---

* In addition to being one of the patron saints of Italy, Francis is also the patron of Catholic Action, merchants and, more recently, ecologists.

** St. Francis is credited with introducing the Christmas crib or crèche, an artistic re-creation of the stable in Bethlehem, with Mary, Joseph, the baby Jesus, angels, shepherds, and so on.

We are drawn to the many stories of Il Poverello, "the little poor one," because of their grace and simplicity. There is joy, compassion, even humour here. After all, who doesn't want to hear about a saint who danced in front of the Pope, listened to angel musicians, tended lepers, debated with the sultan, restored churches and asked for almond pastries on his deathbed? The all-consuming love of God that lay behind all his actions, whether noble or childlike, is Francis' most important legacy to his many admirers today.*

* 1982 marked the 800th anniversary of Francis' birth. That year five million pilgrims visited Assisi.

St. Teresa of Avila

1515-1581

October 15

The time is the Renaissance. Shakespeare is busy writing his soon-to-be-famous plays in England; Michelangelo is struggling with his paints in the Sistine Chapel; court musicians from one end of Europe to another are experimenting with the new chansons, madrigals and fantasias.

The time is also the Reformation. The same societies that take such delight in the stagecraft of the theatre, the brilliant frescoes and the new musical forms are also being threatened by an upheaval in religious thought on a nearly unparalleled scale. Martin Luther's challenge to the established order took its first official step when he nailed his 95 Theses to the door of Wittenberg Cathedral in 1517, two years after Teresa de Cepeda was born in Avila. The world has not been the same since.

This Renaissance, the enthusiastic rebirth of the human spirit through the new attitudes found in culture and learning, also proved to be the ideal environment in which to nurture the works of those marked out by genius. Dramatic political gestures, intensely creative ideas in art, brilliant scientific theories – all these wondrous additions to the way society viewed itself flourished in a climate made for innovation.

Likewise, this Reformation involved many fiercely committed souls in an often violent struggle to confront the abuses that had crept into a system unchallenged for centuries and which was now an easy target for those who had finally found a voice with which to call out for reform.

Teresa of Avila certainly belongs to the parade of outstanding men and women we see striding forcefully across every sixteenth-century landscape. Unlike some of her fellows, however, her life was not devoted to originality and innovation, for the goal she had in mind was a return to a set of clearly articulated values established centuries before. After twenty-five years in a Spanish Carmelite convent, she painfully realized that the initial aims of her order – penance, contemplation, personal sanctity – had been eroded after centuries of neglect and complacency.

The vigorous if misguided opposition raised against her attempts at reform proved futile, and eventually she was allowed to found her own convents and monasteries in keeping with the original ideals of the order. Her new establishments became known as "Discalced" Carmelites, to signify those whose poverty and humility sends them out into the world "without shoes."

Teresa's "reformation" was carried out under the chilling shadow of the Spanish Inquisition. She herself spent two years of her life under arrest; her visions and mystical experiences were scorned and refuted by many of her colleagues and superiors. These setbacks did not seem to slow her down, for her own spiritual "rebirth" gave her much strength. And in the true Renaissance spirit, Teresa was a woman of many talents. In a vigorous, earthy Spanish she wrote poems, letters, works of devotion; as she was fond of saying, only those who liked to eat, sleep and laugh could enter her order. All the while she travelled through Spain and worked for the establishment of her new houses.

Like Catherine of Siena, the only other female Doctor of the Church, Teresa was able to combine a deeply mystical interior life with a hard-headed practical involvement in everyday events. And like the great artists of genius who lived alongside her in a century of Renaissance and Reformation, her works – both her religious order and her writings – have lived on. They continue to inspire those seeking spiritual understanding 400 years later.*

---

* George Eliot draws on the figure of Teresa in the introduction to *Middlemarch*, her masterpiece of nineteenth-century fiction. Francis Poulenc uses a true story of courage and sacrifice during the French Revolution in his twentieth-century opera, *Dialogue of the Carmelites*.

All Saints' Day

November 1

Saints come in all shapes and sizes. Some are famous for their piety, religious fervour or mystical experiences; others came to public notice for their heroic fortitude in martyrdom; a few can also be described as cantankerous,* ambitious and downright worldly. And since the tradition of honouring special people after their deaths has its roots in the very earliest Christian times, the lives of the saints also embrace many hundreds of years of world history and all the varieties of human activity that can be imagined.

To remember St. Thomas More without also thinking of the birth of English humanism, the blossoming of the theatres, and the turmoil of life under Henry VIII is difficult. Likewise, any mention of the Canadian martyrs immediately brings to mind a picture of New France, a vast land unknown to Europeans, covered with virgin forests, untouched and unspoiled. Perhaps this inescapable link to human history is one of the best aspects of the institution of "sainthood": it continually reminds us that there is more to the life of the Church than just the proverbial "here and now."

A multitude of times and places are commemorated in the stories of those who have gone before us; but a close

* St. Jerome was a master of sarcastic insult. He called the unfortunate British monk, Pelagius, a "corpulent dog stuffed with Scottish porridge."

look at the calendar of saints also reveals a staggering range of activities and preoccupations. There is, of course, the church hierarchy, represented by a great number of popes, not surprising considering that most of the first thirty successors to St. Peter were also martyrs. Many founders of religious orders have also been recognized as visionaries and administrators: John Bosco (the Salesians), Angela Merici (the Ursulines), Elizabeth Ann Seaton (Sisters of Charity), Ignatius Loyola (the Jesuits). These men and women created the institutions that brought the Word to countless peoples through schools, monasteries, missions, hospitals. On the other hand, there are also the reformers, people such as John of the Cross who were animated by a desire to renew and revitalize these same institutions when they had somehow drifted away from their original purposes.

We have Doctors of the Church, intellectual figures of gigantic stature such as Basil, Ambrose and Anselm, those whose writings have been studied for centuries, perhaps with debate and controversy, but also with respect and admiration. At the same time, others lived in obscurity, humble and poor, people like Isidore the farmer; Paschal Baylon, the door keeper; Benedict Joseph Labre, a beggar; Zita, a servant.

Edmund Campion, the English Jesuit who was martyred during the Reformation struggles; Elizabeth of Hungary, the young noblewoman who devoted her life to the care of the poor after the death of her husband; Louis IX, the French king who went on crusade and created the exquisite Sainte Chapelle in Paris as a reliquary for the crown of thorns that he brought home; a sixteenth-century Peruvian nun, Rose of Lima, who lived a life of great sanctity amid suffering – the catalogue of saints goes on and on.

Today we are joined to all these holy, interesting, admirable, eccentric, difficult or inspiring people not because of some bureaucratic canonization process that has put an official seal of approval on them, but through the life of Christ who has called us across the ages to be sisters and brothers together in our shared faith in him, our sustaining hope for salvation, and our enduring love for one another.*

---

* The process of officially recognizing a saint is called canonization. It is a long, drawn out procedure lasting years, even decades, and involves a very detailed study of the life history of the person under investigation. Near the very end of the many stages towards sainthood, the person may be called "Blessed" or "Venerable." Butler's *Lives of the Saints* contains over two thousand entries.

All Souls' Day

November 2

The rituals surrounding the mystery of death are many and varied. Human societies do not merely discard the remains of their members as so much unwanted rubbish; reverence for the dead is a major aspect of our behaviour that distinguishes us from our ape-like pre-human ancestors. In fact, the flowers present at a Neanderthal burial site were part of the evidence that scientists used to decide that these stocky cave dwellers were really true cousins of the modern human race.

Some cultures have made a highly elaborate religion out of death, notably the ancient Etruscans and Egyptians. Even the youngest schoolchild is familiar with the mummies now found in museums everywhere but originally buried with an extravagant collection of everyday items in rock tombs and pyramids. Likewise, anthropologists and historians have made us familiar with a multitude of other funerary customs: the Parsi Towers of Silence in India; the Anglo-Saxon ship burials that have revealed such fabulous hoards of gold and jewellery; the North American Indian graves frequently unearthed during construction work; the funeral pyres of devout Hindus set alight and adrift in the Ganges; the Chinese tombs which are also storehouses of artistic treasure.

No one has succeeded, however, in removing our justifiable and entirely human fear of this last journey. As someone remarked, "Everyone is afraid of dying; no one is afraid of being dead."* And many of our customs have evolved out of a desire to ease this transition for all concerned, especially the bereaved ones left behind. But however glowingly memorialized and satisfactorily mourned the dearly departed may be, eventually time passes, the floral tributes fade, the tombstones become worn and weathered and no one remembers us any longer.

Today, however, is the day officially, specifically, set aside for remembering: our own family and friends who have gone before us, of course, but also the legions of others whom we never knew, over countless ages of time, however far away or incomprehensible their lives might be to us. For those who have shared this world of ours – who once enjoyed the flowers on a spring day; who listened to the birdsong on a morning long ago; who watched the same stars as we do on a crisp winter night – we turn our minds and hearts today in a prayer that embraces all humanity. As St. Ambrose said, "We have loved them in life, let us not forget them in death."**

---

* This is a modern version of the saying, "The ancients dreaded death; the Christian can only fear dying," attributed to Julius Hare (1795-1855).

** The doctrine of Purgatory recognizes the fact that we may not be ready for God when he is ready for us. Somehow, we may need some further growth and purification at the end of our earthly lives before we can be fully in harmony with our creator. The Council of Trent stated that the prayers of the living can influence the process by which those already gone before us are arriving at their final destination in God's kingdom. The doctrine was reaffirmed by Pope Paul VI in 1968 and by the Congregation for the Doctrine of the Faith in 1979.

St. Cecilia's Day

November 22

St. Cecilia, the traditional patron of music, is one of the many early Roman martyrs about whom history says little. To remedy this lamentable state of affairs, later pious biographers added picturesque and edifying details for their eager, but credulous, audiences. That she founded a church in Trastevere; that she was buried in a very special and honoured place in the Christian cemetery; that her companions in martyrdom are historically verifiable personages – these meagre facts seem to be the extent of our knowledge of St. Cecilia. By 545 A.D., a narrative of her passion had "emerged," and since the sixteenth century she has been honoured as the special patron saint of music. This attribution in turn seems to derive from the legend that she sang to God in her heart while angels playing various instruments provided the music for her wedding. St. Cecilia's emblem in art is an organ, of the small portable kind.

Whatever St. Cecilia did in her life, we are nevertheless grateful to have this day dedicated to her, because if there is one organization on earth that deserves a patron of music, it is the Church. The list of important Christian figures who also find their way into every standard history of music is overwhelming. Besides Gregory the Great, whose contributions are mentioned elsewhere in these pages, the list of gifted composers, performers, theoreticians and choirmasters who were involved in providing music for worship over the centuries seems endless.

First on our list of apprentices to the Patron of Music* might be St. Ambrose, bishop of Milan. It was said that his hymns were so ravishing that converts came into the Church just to hear them. We know of Guido D'Arezzo, an eleventh-century monk in central Italy whose teaching methods paved the way for the whole system of musical notation that students now know (and perhaps love). There is Abbess Hildegard von Bingen, mediaeval poet, mystic and composer; her works are treasured by early music enthusiasts today, 800 years after her death. Our list could also include Michael Praetorius, prolific sixteenth-century composer, historian of music, and priest; William Byrd, devout Catholic whose talent and discretion helped him keep both his head and his job in Protestant England; Alfonso X, "The Wise," of Castile, responsible for the dozens of cantigas in praise of the Virgin. All these are worthy of our remembrance this day.

And on and on the music plays, taking in the great masses, the sacred cantatas and the solemn vespers; through the famous baroque oratorios such as "Messiah"; including all the hymns, carols and anthems; eventually bringing us round to black American spirituals, gospel

* The patron of music has in turn been recognized by a number of works composed in her honour. Handel and Purcell both wrote odes to mark this day; there are masses for St. Cecilia by Haydn and Gounod. In 1942 Benjamin Britten wrote a hymn in her honour with text by W. H. Auden.

choirs, Salvation Army bands and a million other forms, as each generation seeks advances and developments in the theory and practice of music. Many of these are related to the production of sacred music and directly inspired by the never-changing desire to glorify the Lord, singing a new song.

Christ the King

Last Sunday of the liturgical year

He has been acclaimed the world's greatest teacher, the last of the prophets, the liberator of the poor. His detractors have accused him of blasphemy, political instigation, out-and-out chicanery. In his name, wars have been fought, countries ravaged, crusades unleashed. In his name, schools have been built, hospitals founded, the hungry fed. We call him our brother, our saviour, our friend.

Whenever we try to describe him, whether to ourselves or to the rest of the world, we find it difficult to set our faith free from the weight of history and the burden it imposes on our belief. Can we thread our way back through tradition, philosophy and theology to find the one whom we honour today in his glory, the king who has the final claim on our love, our fidelity and our worship? Even if we return to sacred scripture and, with the utmost care and sincerity, read and study every line, we can never totally understand him. The limitations of every human language are never more apparent than when we attempt to capture him on paper. However hard we try, with all the means of art and scholarship at our disposal, the picture that emerges is always blurred and indistinct, giving us some idea of the man we think we might know, and only the shadow of the God we want to love.

Our imaginations have been forever shaped by Michelangelo's painting in the Sistine Chapel, showing the Father as a vigorous old man sitting up in the clouds and surrounded by angels. Our ability to conjure up the Son has likewise been unconsciously influenced by the thousands of works that were inspired by piety and supposed to convey his spiritual beauty to his sentimental flock. No matter; the face that we seek in our struggle to invoke his humanity is hardly important. In the final analysis, most of our understanding about his divinity can be little more than words on a page, phrases lifted from a textbook, mere logical formulas that can never satisfy our deepest inner longings.

What are we waiting for when we pray for him to come again in glory? We cannot imagine or understand all that is meant by that simple phrase "the end of the world." Do we envisage a well-run Kingdom of the Righteous, ourselves included of course, the enemies of humanity suitably punished, and all made new again and perfect? We do not know.

But nevertheless something in our very nature compels us to turn ourselves towards him, sometimes readily, sometimes with hesitation, in some sort of acknowledgment of ourselves as his humble servants. In this sense, everything in our lives – what we do, why we worship, how we think – is related to the overwhelming fact of our relationship to him.

And sometimes we put aside the words and images that make him real and understandable to us in our human limitations: the suffering servant, the good shepherd, the light of the world. We put aside the notion of him enthroned somewhere waiting to judge us and looking with stern disfavour at our inevitable weakness and foolishness. We put these all aside, not to forget about them, but for one brief moment to forget ourselves, and look beyond, not to another world, but to his presence in this one. And his nearness so honours and moves our hearts that the only worship we can offer to such a king is contained in the simplest prayer: "My Lord and my God."

Printed in Canada
Imprimerie Gagné Ltée